"America's leading source of self-help legal information." ✯

—Yahoo!

LEGAL [illegible]N
ONLINE ANYTIME

24 hours a day

www.nolo.com

AT THE NOLO.COM SELF-HELP LAW CENTER, YOU'LL FIND

- **Nolo's comprehensive Legal Encyclopedia filled with plain-English information on a variety of legal topics**
- **Nolo's Law Dictionary—legal terms without the legalese**
- **Auntie Nolo—if you've got questions, Auntie's got answers**
- **The Law Store—over 250 self-help legal products including: Downloadable Software, Books, Form Kits and eGuides**
- **Legal and product updates**
- **Frequently Asked Questions**
- **NoloBriefs, our free monthly email newsletter**
- **Legal Research Center, for access to state and federal statutes**
- **Our ever-popular lawyer jokes**

Quality Law Books & Software for Everyone

Nolo's user-friendly products are consistently first-rate. Here's why:

- A dozen in-house legal editors, working with highly skilled authors, ensure that our products are accurate, up-to-date and easy to use
- We continually update every book and software program to keep up with changes in the law
- Our commitment to a more democratic legal system informs all of our work
- We appreciate & listen to your feedback. Please fill out and return the card at the back of this book.

Our "No-Hassle" Guarantee

Return anything you buy directly from Nolo for any reason and we'll cheerfully refund your purchase price. No ifs, ands or buts.

Read This First

The information in this book is as up-to-date and accurate as we can make it. But it's important to realize that the law changes frequently, as do fees, forms, and procedures. If you handle your own legal matters, it's up to you to be sure that all information you use—including the information in this book—is accurate. Here are some suggestions to help you:

First, make sure you've got the most recent edition of this book. To learn whether a later edition is available, check the edition number on the book's spine and then go to Nolo's online Law Store at www.nolo.com or call Nolo's Customer Service Department at 800-728-3555.

Next, even if you have a current edition, you need to be sure it's fully up-to-date. The law can change overnight. At www.nolo.com, we post notices of major legal and practical changes that affect the latest edition of a book. To check for updates, find your book in the Law Store on Nolo's website (you can use the "A to Z Product List" and click the book's title). If you see an "Updates" link on the left side of the page, click it. If you don't see a link, that means we haven't posted any updates. (But check back regularly.)

Finally, we believe accurate and current legal information should help you solve many of your own legal problems on a cost-efficient basis. But this text is not a substitute for personalized advice from a knowledgeable lawyer. If you want the help of a trained professional, consult an attorney licensed to practice in your state.

1st edition

Becoming a Mediator

Your Guide to Career Opportunities

by Attorney-Mediators Peter Lovenheim
& Emily Doskow

First Edition	AUGUST 2004
Editor	EMILY DOSKOW
Book Design	SUSAN PUTNEY
Cover Design	SUSAN PUTNEY
Production	SUSAN PUTNEY
Proofreading	ROBERT WELLS
Index	THÉRÈSE SHERE
Printing	DELTA PRINTING SOLUTIONS, INC.

Lovenheim, Peter.

Becoming a mediator : your guide to career opportunities / by Peter Lovenheim and Emily Doskow.-- 1st ed.

p. cm.

ISBN 1-4133-0077-4

1. Conflict management--Vocational guidance--United States. 2. Mediation--Vocational guidance--United States. 3. Dispute resolution (Law)--Vocational guidance--United States. I. Doskow, Emily. II. Title.

HM1126.L683 2004

303.6'9'02373--dc22

2004049537

For information on bulk purchases or corporate premium sales, please contact the Special Sales Department. For academic sales or textbook adoptions, ask for Academic Sales. Call 800-955-4775 or write to Nolo, 950 Parker Street, Berkeley, CA 94710.

Dedication

To Jan Goldberg.

P.L.

Acknowledgments

Thank you to Andrew Thomas, executive director of the Center for Dispute Settlement in Rochester, New York, for giving me the opportunity nearly 20 years ago to be trained as a mediator and later to join the staff. Thanks also to the current training staff for allowing me to observe recent training sessions.

Thank you to the many mediators, professors, administrators, and others who spoke with me about their work and who allowed me to include their comments in this book, and especially to Jim Melamed of Mediate.com. Jim's knowledge of the mediation field and his insight into the experience of being a mediator were of great help.

Many thanks to Emily Doskow for a superb job of updating, expanding, and improving this book, and to researcher Ella Hirst, editor Lisa Guerin, editor Janet Portman, and publisher Jake Warner.

To Jan Goldberg: thank you for helping me keep at it and for being such a good friend. And finally, to my children, Sarah, Val, and Ben: I've said it before, but it's worth repeating: may all your disputes be little ones.

P.L.

Thanks are due to many who helped complete the new incarnation of this book at Nolo. Enormous thanks to Ella Hirst, whose thorough and wonderfully nitpicky research assistance was invaluable, and to Lisa Guerin, whose lighthanded and careful editing contributed greatly to this edition.

Many thanks to James MacPherson of National Mediation for bringing to life the section on ombudsman work in Chapter 7 and for offering his perspective on becoming a mediator.

As always, I'm enormously grateful to Mady Shumofsky, mediator/facilitator/trainer extraordinaire—specifically, for her help with Chapter 7 and other parts of the book, and generally, for being the most insightful, intelligent, and supportive friend and colleague I can imagine.

This book would not exist without the fine original text by Peter Lovenheim, and all credit is due to him for the strong foundation on which this edition is built.

E.D.

Table of Contents

3 Where Mediators Work

4 Mediator Training and Education

5 Job Opportunities in Mediation

6 Job Opportunities in Mediation Support

7 Job Opportunities in Mediation-Related Fields

Introduction

There's a cartoon that illustrates a lot of what's wrong with our legal system. It shows two men in business suits seated on a park bench. Their suits are muddied and torn; they look like bums. One turns to the other and says, sadly, "We should have gone to mediation."

We're meant to understand that the two men had knocked heads together in a lawsuit, and had both been ruined. They could have been business partners, an employee and his boss, neighbors, even former friends. They could be any two people caught in a dispute—and then caught again in the adversarial legal system.

In recent years, increasing numbers of Americans—in fact, people all over the world—have caught on that not all conflict has to end in court. Instead, more and more people are trying to work out solutions to their disputes with the aid of trained, neutral third parties: mediators. Across the country, hundreds of thousands of cases have been successfully resolved through mediation, and mediation continues to grow in popularity as a way to resolve conflict.

Not surprisingly, as people experience mediation, many become curious about whether they too could become mediators. Mediation careers have natural appeal to therapists, social workers, human resources professionals, retired judges, and—perhaps more than anyone else—disenchanted lawyers.

This book is for anyone who is considering becoming a mediator—whether you are a community volunteer, a therapist, a social worker, a human resources director, or a lawyer. The book is designed to help the least experienced to the most sophisticated reader get a clear sense of the field.

Motives for Mediating

As a profession, mediation is still relatively new, and there is no one single career path. Building a career as a mediator isn't easy—it requires knowledge of the field, some creativity, and lots of dedication and perseverance. Nevertheless, more and more people every year decide to give it a try.

Do they do it for the money? A few people make more than a million dollars a year mediating. Others earn six-figure incomes. But mediators who become rich are the exception. Most are fortunate to earn a good living, and many find that they need to supplement their mediation practice with teaching, training, facilitation, or other pursuits.

How about for the prestige? Some prominent mediators—former president Jimmy Carter, for example—enjoy worldwide esteem for their accomplishments as peacemakers. But for the most part, mediators labor out of the limelight and receive very little recognition for their work.

The real motivation usually lies elsewhere. In most cases, mediators are driven by something nobler than a desire for wealth or recognition: a deeply felt need to be of service, to use one's skills to accomplish something of value, to connect with other people, and to make a difference in their lives.

Listen to the words of some mediators: "Most people, after doing their first mediation, levitate for a time. Your hat size grows threefold, you feel wonderful and want to do nothing but mediate for the rest of your career." That's Mark Appel, senior vice president of the American Arbitration Association (AAA). Any of dozens of other mediators we know might say the same thing.

Dolly Hinckley, a divorce mediator, says: "I've met some really nice people from doing this work—people who are really concerned about their children and who want to do what's best for their spouse. . . . I like being the one to help them. I don't think I'm ever going to retire."

And consider this from Chris Kauders, a lawyer-turned-mediator who, through his company Pre-Trial Solutions, Inc., in Boston, mediates personal injury and employment cases: "I love it. I love helping the parties solve the disputes. It's tiring. It can be grueling. But I love it."

And finally, from Don Reder, commercial mediator and president of Dispute Resolution, Inc., in Hartford, Connecticut: "I think it's the best job in the world. I love it. I hope I can keep doing it until it's time for me to check out."

Helping people resolve conflict is sacred work, and most mediators are drawn to the work for precisely this reason. A few may become rich, and a handful receive wide praise, but all mediators—from the volunteer helping neighbors settle a dispute over a shared driveway, to the family mediator helping a couple cooperate for the sake of their children, to the commercial mediator helping companies preserve a business relationship—are sustained by rewards beyond money, praise, or fame.

We're pleased to be able to offer, through this book, a road map to this exciting—and rewarding—career. It can be a challenge to find your way in this new field, to find your niche and then to become successful. But if you persevere, you will be glad you made the journey.

Challenges in the Mediation Field

Mediation is still an evolving field. Just as you will need to find your niche within the field, mediation is still finding its niche within our society. Here are a few of the challenges mediators face.

First, in some practice areas and in some communities, there seem to be more mediators than disputes to resolve. Actually, the problem isn't that there aren't enough disputes—human beings produce them in ample numbers, and the courts are clogged with them. It's just that many people are still not aware of mediation as an option. The real challenge is getting people to bring their disputes to mediation.

Mediation is now mandatory, by law, for certain types of cases. So if you work as a salaried mediator with a government program, this problem won't usually affect you. However, if you are a mediator in private practice, you may need to be constantly drumming up business in order to get enough cases through the door. As Don Reder, president of Dispute Resolution, Inc., observes, "If you're going the independent route—setting up a practice as an independent mediator—you have to be prepared to do relentless marketing. The truth is, it's harder sometimes to get cases than to settle cases."

Another concern in the mediation field is the role of lawyer-mediators. In the early years of mediation—the 1970s and 1980s—the organized bar largely scoffed at mediation, as if it were an inferior and unworthy method of handling disputes. But as mediation began to catch on—and lawyers themselves gained experience with it—the bar began to view it more favorably.

Now, many lawyers take mediator training and make themselves available to mediate cases. Some state courts and legislatures allow only lawyers to mediate certain types of cases that are referred by the courts. As a result, some state and federal government programs now either exclude nonlawyers from mediating or give preference to lawyer-mediators. Also, many lawyers, when they refer clients to mediation, have a bias in favor of choosing mediators who are lawyers. This is a problem for mediators who don't have advanced degrees and who must market even harder to get business.

To be sure, there are times when a mediator's effectiveness is enhanced by a knowledge of the law and local legal customs. However, a legal background by itself does not make someone a good mediator. The role of lawyer-mediators is a contentious issue within the mediation field and one that is not likely to be resolved soon. Still, as mediation grows, so do opportunities for mediators with different types of training.

Job Opportunities

If you happen to be a lawyer, there are definitely job opportunities available to you as a mediator. If you are not a lawyer, you can still find work—and this book will help you in your search. For example, the new area of online mediation appears to offer good opportunities for mediators who are not lawyers. Also, mediation support jobs and jobs in related fields like facilitation and ombuds work don't require a law degree.

Sometimes, a mediator may be chosen precisely because he or she is *not* a lawyer. Moshe Cohen, a businessman who became a mediator in Cambridge, Massachusetts, explains: "All these other attorney-mediators are connected to the legal community in ways I'm never going to be, but a lot of business people don't like lawyers and are glad to use a businessperson as a mediator if they know one."

Whatever your background—law, social work, teaching, psychology, business, homemaking, or parenting—if you have the skills and desire, we believe you can become a mediator and find a satisfying career.

Overview of the Book

This book can help you decide whether you want to become a mediator—and if you do, what steps you can take to move your new career along. In Chapter 1, you will learn exactly what mediation is. Chapter 2 will help you think about whether you would make a good mediator. Chapter 3 provides more specific information about where mediators work. Chapter 4 discusses training options, Chapter 5 gives details on jobs in mediation, and Chapters 6 and 7 describe a number of mediation support and mediation-related jobs.

If you decide to become a mediator, not only will you have the opportunity to develop a good career but also, in a society that is increasingly fragmented and violent, you will have the personal satisfaction of becoming a diplomat for peace. And you can use those skills wherever you go.

We hope this book helps you begin. ●

What Is Mediation?

To mediate means "to go between" or "to be in the middle." This, literally, is what mediators do. They go between people involved in a dispute and try to help them work out a solution to their problem.

Unlike a judge or an arbitrator, who listens to evidence and then imposes a decision on the parties, a mediator can't tell the participants what to do. Instead, the mediator's role is to help the participants communicate with each other, consider their dispute from different perspectives, and try to come up with a resolution that works for everyone.

You may have picked up this book because you are interested in mediation, but don't know much about it or about what mediators actually do. This chapter gets down to basics by explaining what mediation is and how it works—and giving examples of the disputes that mediators help people resolve. We'll compare mediation to some of the other methods of resolving disputes, give a brief history of mediation in the United States, and describe a typical mediation session.

If you are already mediating cases and just want to know more about building a mediation practice or about jobs in the mediation field, you probably can skip this chapter. However, if you are new to mediation, even if you have some experience, you might want to review the material here.

A. The Mediator's Role

A mediator's only role is to work with parties to help them evaluate their goals and options and find their own solution to whatever problem is causing conflict between them. The mediator is not like a judge deciding who is right and who is wrong. Mediators don't give legal advice, even if they happen to be lawyers, and most mediators don't act as counselors or therapists (unless the parties purposely hire a therapist-mediator).

Exactly how a mediator helps parties reach a solution may be puzzling to those who aren't familiar with the process. Although each of us acts, at times, as a mediator—department heads mediate between workers; parents mediate between children; friends mediate between friends—most of us would not attempt to sit down in a room with total strangers and, in the course of an hour or two (or a day or two), try to help them find a solution to a problem that has vexed them for months or years.

Formal mediation involves a lot more than just getting folks together to talk about their problem. The work of the mediator, who is trained in conflict resolution, is central to the process, and it is helped along by the structure of the mediation session—a highly ritualized, multistage proceeding.

Employing their skills through the different stages of mediation, mediators work to help the parties

- identify the true issues involved in their dispute
- understand the difference between what they want and what they need
- understand the wants and needs of the other side, and
- consider the possible options realistically.

If the mediator can help the parties do these things, the parties will most likely reexamine their previously fixed positions and become more open to a broader range of solutions.

History and Growth of Mediation

In eastern cultures, mediation has long been the preferred method of resolving disputes. In Japan, where there are said to be more flower arrangers than lawyers, mediation is used as a matter of course. In China, it is estimated that 35 times as many disputes are settled through mediation as through the courts; some 800,000 mediation panels operate at local and regional levels, with more than one million people trained as mediators.

Even in the United States, mediation has a long history. In 1636, the Puritan founders of Dedham (a community located southwest of Boston) provided in their covenant for a system of informal mediation. In New Netherland, Dutch colonists established a Board of Nine Men to serve as "friendly mediators and arbitrators." In colonial Virginia, the legislature noted the "excessive charges and greate delaies" of litigation and encouraged citizens to resolve disputes by other means.

Later, beginning in the 1800s, Chinese immigrants on the West Coast, Scandinavian immigrants in the Midwest, and Jewish immigrants in New York set up mediation boards to resolve disputes within their own communities.

In 1947, the federal government established the Federal Mediation and Conciliation Service (FMCS) to resolve disputes between industry and labor, and in 1964, the U.S. Department of Justice formed the Community Relations Service to mediate racial disputes arising under the Civil Rights Act.

In the early 1970s, state and federal courts were faced with increasing numbers of lawsuits over consumer issues, civil rights, product liability, personal injuries, and more. In an early effort to address delays caused by this backlog, the U.S. Department of Justice conducted an experiment to find out whether disputes involving ordinary citizens could be successfully resolved through mediation as an alternative to traditional litigation. During a 15-month test period in the late 1970s, 3,947 disputes were handled by locally based mediation centers in Atlanta, Kansas City, and Los Angeles.

Of the cases that went to a formal mediation session, more than 82% were successfully resolved. As many as 95% were resolved for some types of disputes. Since then, the federal Administrative Dispute Resolution Act and scores of state laws have been passed to establish, fund, and promote the use of mediation in an ever-increasing range of circumstances.

At the same time, the private sector has spawned hundreds of national, regional, and local for-profit dispute resolution services, as well as thousands of independent private mediators. Mediation continues to grow in popularity every year—and more and more job opportunities are created.

B. Qualities of Mediation

There are many different ways of resolving legal or interpersonal disputes. Each has different positive and negative qualities—although we believe, of course, that mediation's many benefits make it a good dispute resolution choice for most situations. In this section we compare mediation to other forms of dispute resolution and discuss exactly what makes mediation such an effective way to resolve conflict.

1. Mediation Compared to Arbitration and Litigation

People often confuse the words *mediation, arbitration,* and *litigation*—and *meditation.* Co-author Peter Lovenheim was introduced on a national talk show once as an expert on how to resolve disputes through meditation! But the words themselves sound more alike than the procedures they describe actually are. Let's take a quick look at the three major dispute resolution processes—leaving meditation for a different book—and how they differ.

Litigation: In litigation, parties go to court to have a judge or jury decide their respective rights under the law. Parties usually hire lawyers to guide them through the legal action and to speak for them in court. Throughout the process, strict rules limit the information and documents the parties may present, as well as what they can say to try to prove their case. These are called rules of evidence. Typically in litigation, one side wins and the other side loses, although the losing side can ask a higher court to change the decision in what is called an appeal. If a court orders one side to pay money or take other actions, the order can be enforced by marshals, police, or other government agencies.

Arbitration: Arbitration is like going to a private court with more relaxed rules. It has long been used to resolve commercial and labor disputes (including, more recently, labor disputes in professional sports). In arbitration, a neutral third party—the arbitrator—conducts a hearing between the disputants and then, acting as a judge, makes a decision that is legally binding on everyone involved. Arbitration is less formal than litigation, and strict rules of evidence are not usually followed. Partly for this reason, cases tend to move through arbitration much more quickly than they do through court proceedings. Usually, parties agree in advance that the arbitrator's decision will be binding, meaning that it cannot be overturned except in rare circumstances (for example, if the arbitrator is later found to have been biased either in favor of or against one of the parties).

Mediation: In mediation, the neutral mediator does not act as a judge or arbitrator, and has no authority to impose a decision. Instead, the mediator meets with the disputants face to face and helps them work out their own solution to their dispute by listening, questioning, negotiating, and creating options. This process will be described in much more detail later.

Compromise is often involved in mediation, but not in the sense of just splitting the difference between the parties' positions. The goal of mediation is to find a win-win solution in which both sides achieve something they want. Rules of evidence and other formal procedures are not normally used in mediation, but if the parties reach an agreement they can make it legally binding by having it drafted in the form of a contract.

The chart below reiterates some of the differences among mediation, arbitration, and litigation.

Qualities of Mediation, Arbitration, and Litigation

Process	Mediation	Arbitration	Litigation
Who decides?	Parties	Arbitrator	Judge or jury
Who controls?	Parties	Arbitrator and attorneys	Judge and attorneys
Procedure	Informal	Somewhat Formal	formal
Time to decisive hearing	Weeks	Months	Years
Cost to party	Nominal or low	Moderate	Significant
Rules of evidence	None	Informal	Complex
Publicity	Private	Usually private	Public
Relations of parties	Cooperation may increase	Antagonistic	Antagonistic
Focus	Future	Past	Past
Method of negotiation	Compromise	Hard bargaining	Hard bargaining
Communication	Often improved	Blocked	Blocked
Goal	Win-Win	Win-Lose	Win-Lose
Compliance	Generally honored	Often resisted or appealed	Often resisted or appealed

Source: Adapted from Cloke and Strachan, "Mediation and Prepaid Legal Plans," *Mediation Quarterly*, 1987, 18, 94.

Other Methods of Dispute Resolution

In addition to arbitration and litigation, there are a number of ways other than mediation that parties can use to try to resolve disputes. Some involve only the parties who are having the dispute, and others use the assistance of third parties. These include:

- **Negotiation:** Parties try to resolve their dispute by talking directly with each other or negotiating through their lawyers, without filing a lawsuit.
- **Conciliation:** A neutral third party intervenes to reduce tensions and get the parties talking—often helping them get to a point where they can either negotiate the issue themselves or decide on a means of dispute resolution.
- **Fact-finding:** A neutral third party—often an expert in the matter under dispute—assesses the issues and presents findings of fact and recommendations to the parties. When used in cases that are already in litigation, this process is sometimes also known as early neutral evaluation.
- **Collaborative law:** In a family law case, both parties hire lawyers who agree to work collaboratively toward a resolution, without going to court. If the case proceeds to litigation, both parties have to hire new lawyers and start all over again.

A trained mediator can assist with negotiation or conciliation, and can perform a fact-finding or neutral evaluation function in appropriate situations. Some lawyer-mediators who represent clients practice collaborative law.

2. Mediation Is Flexible and Forward Looking

Almost any kind of dispute can be mediated. Mediation can be used to decide who will own the Sinai Peninsula or how you and your next door neighbor will share your common driveway. It can be used to determine how one computer company will compensate another for infringing on a copyright or how your dry cleaner will compensate you for losing your favorite sweater. It can be a way to determine whether a shelter for the homeless can be operated by a church in a residential neighborhood or in whose home your children should live after you and your spouse divorce.

For these and many other types of disputes, mediation works well because it is forward looking, not backward looking. The law looks back to find who was right and who was wrong in events that already happened. Mediation looks ahead to find a solution both parties can live with going forward.

3. Mediation Is Empowering and Satisfying

In formal legal proceedings, the court uses its power to dictate a decision. In mediation, people empower themselves to find their own solutions. This may help explain why mediation has taken hold and is gaining so fast in popularity—both as a means of dispute resolution and as a career choice. Many people wonder why it should take two to three years to get a result in a simple legal claim, and why people should tolerate an experience where, to paraphrase mediator and scholar Jerold S. Auerbach, they don't understand the procedures or the language, an attorney assumes the role of parent and the disputant becomes a dependent child, and the judge looms as a menacing authority figure, empowered to divest litigants of property or liberty.

Studies have demonstrated that mediation has an enormously high satisfaction rate among participants—in part, because they have the power to shape the proceedings and determine the outcome. Following the mediation studies discussed above in "History and Growth of Mediation," six-month follow-up interviews with the disputants showed very high rates of satisfaction with mediation, as detailed in the chart below. In the table, the term *claimant* refers to the person who initiated mediation, and *respondent* refers to the party who agreed to participate.

Disputant Satisfaction for Mediated Cases

Question	Response	Claimant	Respondent
Satisfied with mediation experience?	Yes	88%	88%
	No	9%	8%
	Somewhat	4%	4%
Satisfied with mediation process?	Yes	84%	89%
	No	12%	10%
	Somewhat	3%	5%
Satisfied with mediator?	Yes	88%	88%
	No	8%	7%
	Somewhat	4%	5%
Satisfied with terms of agreement?	Yes	80%	83%
	No	15%	13%
	Somewhat	5%	5%

Source: Cook, Roehl, and Sheppard, *Neighborhood Justice Centers Field Test: Final Evaluation Report, Executive Summary.* Washington, DC: Government Printing Office, 1980, p. 15.

4. When Mediation Makes Sense

Having looked at some of the qualities of mediation and of other dispute resolution procedures, we now take a quick look at the question of what types of cases can or should go to mediation. Certainly, if disputants seek a quick, fair, inexpensive, and flexible solution to their dispute, mediation is often the best bet. But sometimes mediation may not meet the needs of one or more of the parties, or it may be impractical in a particular case.

a. Factors Favoring Mediation

These factors reflect some of mediation's most important benefits, such as speed, privacy, flexibility, and cost savings.

When Direct Negotiations Have Failed, or Are Undesirable or Impossible. In most disputes, direct negotiation between parties without any outside help is the quickest, least expensive, and most private way to resolve the matter. However, if direct talks have failed, then mediation becomes an attractive next step.

Sometimes negotiations would never get started if the parties didn't come to mediation—as where one party is a large corporation that doesn't usually negotiate with individuals and is ignoring the other party's request to discuss the conflict. In this situation, a formal offer to mediate, especially if made through a respected mediation service, may be enough to get the other side's attention.

If one party has poor negotiating skills and knows it, he or she might want to go directly to mediation. The mediator's presence can create a safer environment for discussion, and the mediator can help both parties get their ideas across effectively.

When the Law Cannot Provide a Remedy. Although there are thousands of laws on the books, there are many common disputes for which the law does not provide a remedy. Disputes between family members and between neighbors are often of this type. For example, two sisters who own and run a jewelry store might disagree about who should control different aspects of the business. If they cannot come to terms, the business might fail. Yet there are no legal claims involved—just a dispute between partners that mediation could help settle. In mediation, the more outgoing sister might agree to take on most responsibility for customer service and marketing, while the sister with more technical skills agrees to oversee purchases, manufacturing, and repairs.

When the Parties Want to End a Problem, Not a Relationship. Filing a lawsuit can be a hostile act. When two people already have a strained relationship, filing legal papers will only make it worse. One of the greatest advantages of mediation is that it allows parties to resolve a dispute without destroying their relationship. Many cases involve people who, either by choice or circumstance, want or need to remain on good terms—family members, coworkers, a landlord and tenant, neighbors, or others who have a continuing personal or business relationship. In some cases, the mediation process, with its focus on communication, can help improve a relationship.

When the Dispute Is Private, and the Parties Want to Keep It That Way. Most of what is said or submitted to a court in connection with a lawsuit eventually becomes public record. The only way to keep it private is to get a special order from a judge. To be sure, open courts are important in a democracy because they give the public a chance to see whether prosecutors and judges are doing their jobs well. But reporters who cover the courts know where to find the information that will make an otherwise boring legal story come alive with interesting personal details—and some people have a strong desire to avoid that.

Mediation is a strictly private affair. Mediators are bound to protect the confidences entrusted to them during the mediation sessions; there are no stenographers or tape recorders present. In many states, the law requires that mediation proceedings be confidential.

When the Parties Want to Minimize Costs. Most of the costs in bringing a civil (noncriminal) lawsuit are lawyers' fees. In most major cities today, lawyers' fees range from about $200 to $500 per hour. The median time lawyers spend on a typical civil case, whether in state or federal court, is more than 30 hours. At $150 per hour, that comes to more than $4,500.

In contrast, fees for mediation services range from no charge at nonprofit public mediation centers to $500 or less per party for a half-day session at a typical private mediation service. Even if a party brings a lawyer, the party's cost for the lawyer's fee plus the mediation fee will probably still be much less than if the case had been pursued in court or the lawyer had done all the negotiations from the start.

When the Parties Want to Settle a Dispute Promptly. In some big cities, a litigated case may wait up to five years for trial. Although more than 90% of cases are settled before trial, settlement discussions often do not get serious until a trial date is near. In contrast, at most public mediation centers, mediation sessions are scheduled within a couple of weeks of their submission, and many cases require just one session to reach agreement. Private dispute resolution services take a bit longer because the commercial cases they often handle tend to be more complex. Still, a few months from intake to final resolution would be typical. Even a divorce mediation, which can require a longer process because the parties usually need to gather and consider a significant amount of information, is far quicker than a court dissolution.

b. Factors Opposing Mediation

As valuable as mediation can be, there are still times when it may not be in the best interests of one or both of the parties. For example, when disputants want to establish new legal rights or when a court order is needed immediately to prevent harm, mediation probably isn't the best option. And sometimes, mediation may simply be impossible.

When a Party Wants to Prove the Truth or Set a Legal Precedent. Mediation may resolve a dispute, but it does not result in a judgment for or against either party—or a legal ruling that establishes anyone's rights. Mediated agreements do not establish what happened in the past or say who was right and who was wrong; they relate only to what will happen in the future. Similarly, there are no "test cases" in mediation. That is, you cannot use mediation to establish a legal precedent (a new legal rule) because what is agreed between the parties in one dispute does not affect the parties in any other dispute. So if there is a law someone wants overturned, or if someone needs to prove the truth of something publicly (for example, a woman who has been defamed in the local paper might want to clear her name), this must happen in court rather than in mediation.

And although it doesn't happen often, there are some disputes in which the facts and the law make it clear that one side is completely right and the other completely wrong. In these cases, the person in the right will surely win if the matter goes to court. A person on the right side in such a dispute will be better off bringing a case in court, as long as he or she can tolerate the delays, loss of privacy, and other drawbacks of a lawsuit.

When a Party Wants to Go for the Jackpot. It almost seems to have become an American sport: sue a giant corporation for a huge amount of money, have your lawyer take the case on a contingency fee basis, and hope a sympathetic jury will award you a jackpot.

In fact, not as many people win this legal version of the lottery as it may appear. The press plays it up when a jury awards a plaintiff millions of dollars, but often the judge or an appeals court later substantially reduces the amount. The reduction seldom gets as much publicity as the original award.

People who want to go for a big award against a big company (or even a small company with plenty of insurance) usually choose litigation, not mediation. If they were to mediate, they might get a settlement more quickly and therefore get their money sooner, but because mediation often results in compromise, they would be unlikely to get as much money as if they litigated the claim and carried it all the way to a jury trial. There are no jackpots in mediation—only the certainty of having made an agreement, as opposed to the risk of losing in court (or winning less than you had hoped).

When One Party Is Absent or Incompetent. Mediation normally requires all parties to a dispute to be present for face-to-face discussions. If one or more parties are physically unable to attend—for example, because they are ill, incarcerated, or live at a distance—mediation might not be feasible. Note, however, that sometimes telephone mediation can work, especially as technology improves for picture teleconferencing. Online mediation also offers an option for disputants who are not able to meet physically. (For more about online mediation, see Chapter 5.)

Mediation assumes that both parties are rational and can participate in reasoned discussion and negotiation. If one party is mentally impaired or affected by alcohol or drug abuse, mediation will not work.

Physical impairment, however, usually is no bar to mediation, nor is the fact that someone does not speak English. Many public mediation centers have bilingual staff and also keep a roster of mediators who speak other languages.

When One Party Is Unwilling to Mediate. One side to a dispute simply may have no interest in mediating. A party may genuinely prefer litigation because he or she believes the case in a winner, doesn't perceive enough of an advantage in mediation to consider trying it, or just enjoys the dispute and is in no hurry to end it.

When One Party Needs a Court Order to Prevent Immediate Harm. Some disputes that otherwise could be mediated don't end up there because one party might suffer immediate personal or business harm without an immediate court order. For example, if town officials announce their intention to cut down all the maple trees lining a residential street by next Thursday, neighbors will need to get a judge to issue a court order preventing the town from wielding the ax until the full case can be heard by a court. Once they get the court order stopping the tree choppers, the neighbors may want to ask the judge to put the case on hold while they and town officials try to resolve it through mediation—but not before.

Mediation Where a Crime Has Been Committed

There is debate in the mediation community about whether mediation is appropriate in cases where domestic violence or other forms of abuse are present, or where very serious crimes have been committed. Some people feel that mediation is never appropriate in these cases. Others feel that mediation is structured to lessen the power imbalances created by interpersonal violence, and that safeguards can be put into place that will allow a productive mediation to take place—perhaps even with the result that elements of the abusive relationship will decrease.

Many private mediators don't take on cases that involve criminal conduct. Instead, there are numerous programs that deal specifically with mediation in the criminal law context. Many cities and counties have "VORPs"—Victim-Offender Reconciliation Programs. These usually deal with minor criminal cases like minor harassment, slight property damage, and less serious juvenile cases. Many public mediation centers handle these cases, often under a contract with the local district attorney or court.

There is also an international movement for "restorative justice" that includes a large mediation component, even advocating for the use of mediation in cases of violent crime. In these restorative justice programs, mediations only take place when both offender and victim agree, and when the offender has truly taken responsibility for his or her actions and expressed remorse. The mediation process is usually carefully planned and tightly controlled. Many participants and researchers report powerful results from mediations in this context.

If you plan to become a mediator, you will have to decide what types of cases you want to work on—or are willing to do. Some people may be drawn to VORP or restorative justice work, and others might feel that there's no way that they could be neutral in a situation where a violent crime has been committed. Your only obligation is to engage in an honest self-evaluation to decide what cases you can mediate effectively.

C. Types of Cases Mediators Hear

There's no such thing as a "typical" mediation case. Mediation's flexibility is, after all, one of its greatest strengths. As part of helping you evaluate whether mediation is the right career for you or make a decision about what kind of mediator you want to be, we consider here the kinds of cases mediators actually hear. To put some kind of frame around the picture, we'll divide the types of cases mediators hear into three very broad categories: (1) interpersonal disputes, (2) commercial matters, and (3) public policy issues.

I. Interpersonal Relations

Mediation works especially well with disputes between individuals, particularly when long-term family, work, or neighborhood relationships are involved. A mediator in these cases can help the parties reach below the surface of a dispute to address underlying issues that stress the relationship. The process allows the parties to find ways to relate to each other, even if the break can never be repaired. Examples of these types of cases include:

- **Separation and Divorce:** Divorcing couples mediate issues involving money, property, and children—in these cases, mediation can help the parties save on legal fees and, more importantly, build enough trust to continue parenting their children. The same process can be used by unmarried couples, gay and straight, when relationships end.
- **Newly Established and Intact Relationships:** As an alternative to couples therapy or marriage counseling, couples in an intact marriage or relationship can mediate specific problems in dispute, such as disagreements over child rearing, finances, in-laws, religious practices, and other family obligations. And couples preparing to marry or live together can mediate prenuptial agreements or contracts about how money and property will be shared.

If you are mediating a prenuptial agreement, make sure you have the right resources. Check your state's laws about prenuptial agreements, as laws can be complex and do differ greatly from state to state. For more about prenups, check out *Prenuptial Agreements: How to Write a Fair & Lasting Contract*, by Katherine E. Stoner and Shae Irving (Nolo).

- **General Family Relations:** These cases typically involve disputes between spouses, siblings, or relatives concerning money, inheritances, and sometimes, how the family members relate to one another. Other situations involve family members working in a family business and parents mediating relationship disputes with teenagers or adult children.
- **Business Partner Relations:** Co-owners of a business can mediate issues such as sharing responsibilities within the firm, determining direction or strategy for growth, resolving conflicts in management style, and negotiating terms of an agreement if one partner wants to buy the other out.
- **School Issues:** These cases involve disputes between or among administrators, teachers, students, and parents on matters including academic standards, work conditions, class placement, favoritism, and bullying.
- **Workplace Relations:** Issues for mediation among management and staff include work assignments, wrongful termination, job discrimination, and sexual harassment. Employment-related mediation, facilitation, and training are fast-growing fields with lots of opportunity.
- **Roommate Relations:** College students or adults in shared housing may mediate disputes involving finances, privacy, cleanliness, guests, and noise.
- **Neighbor Relations:** These cases often include matters such as fences, noise, shared driveways, pets, upkeep, and the behavior of children.

2. Commercial Disputes

The term "commercial" is an umbrella classification for all kinds of cases that don't directly relate to interpersonal matters—usually, they involve one or more businesses, or an insurance company dealing with a claim for injury or property damage. In commercial cases, the main issue usually is how much money or property is going to change hands between the parties. The parties, perhaps a merchant and a long-time customer, might have a long-term relationship, or they may be strangers—for example, two motorists in a collision.

Mediation is effective in commercial cases because the parties can be creative and go beyond the strict terms of any legal contract that might be involved. Also, both sides can confide their bottom-line needs to the mediator, who is then in a position to help them work out a mutually satisfying agreement. Examples of commercial disputes include:

- **Small Claims:** These are often claims by a consumer for compensation from a merchant for inadequate goods or services, or claims by merchants for money due from a customer.
- **Landlord-Tenant Disputes:** Tenants mediate demands for improvements to living conditions or return of security deposits. Landlords typically seek overdue rent, changes in a tenant's behavior, or compensation for damage done to the property.
- **Personal Injuries:** These cases usually come to mediation when someone has been injured in a car or other type of accident, and the insurance company and the injured party can't agree on what the injuries are worth.
- **Contract Disputes:** Owners of businesses mediate cases involving many millions of dollars in which claims of breach of contract arise from the manufacture of inadequate goods, negligent construction, or interference with customers. Often these mediations involve multiple parties.

3. Public Policy Disputes

Another area where mediation can be successful in even the most recalcitrant situations is in dealing with political disputes at the community level and far beyond.

Community disputes can be mediated in groups of any size—from small meetings of decisionmakers only, to large meetings open to the public. Determining the location of factories, highways, and new tract homes, deciding how close a homeless shelter will be allowed to a residential neighborhood, setting limits on what type of watercraft may use local waterways and at what speeds, and deciding which organizations may march in a town's official Memorial Day Parade, are all examples of issues of community concern that could be brought to mediation.

Regional disputes can include things like the competing claims to land of Native American tribes and state and county governments, disputed border claims between states, and multistate disputes over water rights.

Mediators also hear international political disputes, such as those involving conflicts among the states of the former Yugoslavia or between countries in the Middle East. One of the best known and probably most successful international mediation efforts was that conducted by former president Jimmy Carter in 1978 between Prime Minister Menachem Begin of Israel and President Anwar

Sadat of Egypt. Carter's 13-day mediation effort at Camp David, the secluded presidential retreat in the Maryland countryside, resulted in the signing of a peace agreement between those two countries that still stands today.

A mediator can also facilitate meetings. Many of the policy disputes described above give rise to large community meetings that aren't necessarily considered mediations, but that require a firm hand to control the process. This is called facilitation, and you'll find more about this mediation-related work in Chapter 7.

4. Focusing Your Mediation Practice

It is conceivable that a skilled mediator could handle almost any type of case because the process of mediation is more or less the same regardless of the type of dispute. In practice, however, many mediators specialize in certain types of cases. For example, mediators with strong interpersonal skills and perhaps a background in social work or psychology might specialize in divorce and family mediation or mediation of disputes between business partners. And a mediator who is also a real estate lawyer might specialize in mediating disputes involving commercial or residential real estate. It would be unusual for the same mediator who hears commercial real estate disputes to also mediate divorces.

You will need to make decisions about what type of mediation suits you best. In reading the descriptions above, were you drawn more to the list of interpersonal disputes, or to the types of disputes under the commercial heading? Did you think it would be exhilarating to mediate with a large community group over important local issues, or did that sound overwhelming to you, while working with a couple in the midst of a breakup sounded right up your alley?

When you first begin mediating, volunteering at a nonprofit public mediation center can be a great way to get exposure to different kinds of cases. This can help you decide where you want to focus your mediation practice—or let you know that you want to be a general mediator, taking in cases in different areas. You will also want to look closely at your own personality traits and skills to see what suits you best. While it's wonderful to challenge yourself by doing new and different things, you needn't go so far that you are completely out of your comfort zone and therefore not enjoying your work!

D. What Mediation Looks Like

The bailiff bangs three times on a table and says, "All Rise! This court is now in session, the Honorable Peter Lovenheim presiding!" If one of us were a judge, that is how a hearing in his or her courtroom might begin.

Mediation begins differently: "Hello. Are you Rebecca Clarence? I'm Peter Lovenheim, the mediator. Will you follow me to the conference room, please?"

Part of the reason for this striking difference between the courtroom and the mediation room is mediation's focus on relationships rather than on formal rules. The relationship between the parties will usually be an important factor in the mediation process. And mediators must establish a trusting relationship with the parties in order to do their job effectively.

Mediation's low-key opening is deceiving—it is really the prelude to a very compelling drama. Remember, mediation is not combat by hired gun like a court trial, and doesn't place the same restrictions on what participants can say. In a mediation session, the disputants themselves—former business partners, angry neighbors, a former employee and the boss who fired her—meet nose-to-nose across the mediation table, with the chance, at last, to say what is on their minds.

If you've never seen a mediation, it may be difficult to picture exactly how it works. After all, there are no weekly television shows about the work of mediators, as there are about lawyers and judges. To understand better what mediation looks like, let's walk through a typical case of the type that might be handled at a nonprofit community mediation center. Many mediators get their first training and experience at these centers (see Chapter 3 for more details). We'll also note some differences between this model and the other models of court-sponsored mediation, mediation with a private, independent mediator, and mediation with a private center.

1. Where the Mediation Is Held

A mediation arranged through a public mediation center is likely to be held at the center's own offices, typically in a downtown office or civic building. It will probably take place in a bare-bones conference room with modest furniture.

Mediations arranged by local and state courts are usually held in conference rooms at the courthouse. When mediations are arranged by private dispute resolution companies, the setting can be plush, such as a big law firm's conference room. And mediators in private practice usually have their own, slightly more modest conference rooms in their offices.

2. Length of Session

Most small, two-party cases—neighborhood disputes, consumer claims, minor business disputes—are mediated in a half day or less; at most they may take a full day. Cases involving more than two parties last longer, as do major commercial disputes (such as complex contract and construction cases); they may last several days, either all in a row or scheduled over a period of weeks. Divorce mediation generally requires a half dozen or more sessions, usually spread over several months. Most nonprofit public mediation centers won't handle complex commercial or divorce cases.

Some nonprofit mediation centers, and most court-sponsored mediation programs, impose time limits on mediation. A two- or three-hour limit, with the option to continue another day if the mediation appears to be productive, would be typical.

3. Agreement to Mediate

Ideally, each of the people involved in a dispute will agree to try mediation. However, this doesn't always happen. Often, by the time one side is thinking about mediation, the relationship is so strained that the parties aren't even speaking to each other. It's fairly common, therefore, for one side to initiate mediation by contacting a mediation service, either public or private, that will then help bring the other party to the table.

If both parties want to mediate, they can hire a private, independent mediator. If there's no need for a mediation service to do the work of getting a reluctant party to the table, the parties have more options, including hiring a mediator who's not affiliated with a mediation service but works independently. Independent mediators usually don't get involved in trying to bring a reluctant party to the table, but mediate cases where both parties are ready to negotiate.

After the first party contacts the mediation service, a case manager there contacts the other side (now designated the *respondent*), by mail or telephone. Occasionally, respondents readily agree to mediate, but often they are reluctant. Sometimes, as we discussed above, they may have good reason to refuse. For example, if they are likely to win in court and have the money and time to see the case through to a verdict, they might decline an overture to mediate. More often, however, respondents hesitate because (1) mediation is unfamiliar and therefore threatening, or (2) they feel so much hostility that they can't stomach the idea of sitting in the same room with their opponent, or (3) a lawyer who is unfamiliar with mediation or who has a negative attitude about it has advised them against it.

Good case managers spend as much time as necessary with respondents to try to overcome their fears and objections to mediation. Often this requires many rounds of phone calls and negotiations concerning exactly what issues will be mediated, who the mediator will be, and when and where the session will be held. (If you want to learn more about what case managers do, Chapter 6 discusses mediation support jobs.)

If and when both sides agree to participate, they will usually be asked to sign an agreement to mediate. This brief document (typically a single page) names the parties and the selected mediator and commits the parties to participate in mediation at the agreed-on time and place, in accordance with the rules and procedures of the mediation service. (For an example of a typical mediation agreement; see below; for a sample set of mediation rules, see Appendix A.)

Below is a sample Agreement to Mediate that is used at a private dispute resolution company.

Agreement to Mediate

Empire Mediation & Arbitration, Inc.

The undersigned agree to have Empire Mediation & Arbitration, Inc. ("Empire") provide mediation services for their dispute.

PURPOSE & RULES: Mediation is a voluntary process in which the mediator helps the parties to reach an agreement about their conflict. The mediator does not have authority to impose a decision or to give legal advice. The hearing is conducted in accordance with Empire's "Commercial Mediation Rules."

MEDIATOR: The parties agree that James C. Moore, Esq., will be the sole Mediator in this case. The Mediator is an independent contractor, not an agent or employee of Empire.

AUTHORITY TO SETTLE: The parties affirm they have authority to act on behalf of the persons or organizations they represent.

FEES: The parties agree to pay mediation fees to Empire in accordance with the attached fee agreement.

LEGAL COUNSEL: The parties have the right to legal counsel and are encouraged to obtain legal advice in connection with this case.

CONFIDENTIALITY: A mediation is a settlement negotiation and is strictly confidential. Statements made in mediation are inadmissible, as provided by law, in future arbitration or court proceedings relating to this dispute. The parties will keep the confidentiality of the mediation and not introduce in any later proceeding statements made by the mediator or the parties, or subpoena a mediator to testify or produce records.

______________________	______________________
Name of Party	Attorney or Representative
______________________	______________________
Name of Party	Attorney or Representative

____

Dated:

4. Who Attends

The people who are directly involved in the dispute must attend the mediation: the neighbors fighting over noise, the boss and the former employee who was terminated, the homeowner and the electrician who did the allegedly faulty wiring. In divorce mediation, of course, the two spouses meet with the mediator.

When parties other than individuals are involved, such as government agencies, insurance companies, or other corporations, it is essential that somebody at the table for each side have authority to settle—in other words, the authority to agree that the agency or company will pay money or take some other action. Otherwise, everyone might spend lots of time and energy hammering out an agreement, only to learn that one party's representative isn't authorized to agree to it.

Lawyers in Mediation

People always have the right to bring a lawyer to mediation, but in most interpersonal disputes and small-business cases, lawyers are not necessary and only increase the cost of the process for the participants. Sometimes, instead of bringing lawyers, parties in these smaller cases bring a friend or relative for moral support. In cases involving substantial amounts of money or significant legal rights, it is common for lawyers to attend. Even then, though, most mediators prefer that lawyers let their clients do much of the talking and function more as advisers than advocates.

For the most part, witnesses are not needed in mediation, because the point of mediation is not to determine what happened in the past but what is going to happen in the future to resolve the dispute. Nevertheless, if parties want to bring witnesses they certainly may ask the mediator. If the mediator agrees, the witnesses generally will attend only part of the session, give the relevant information, and then leave.

5. Physical Setting

The mediator typically greets the parties in a waiting area, conducts them into a conference room, and invites them to take a seat at the table.

The ideal shape for a mediation table is a subject mediators debate vigorously in the pages of professional journals. Some prefer a rectangular table because they believe its resemblance to a typical boardroom table inspires confidence in the mediation process. Others dislike the rectangular table because they think the hard lines encourage inflexible bargaining positions. Some like a square table on the theory that its four equal sides suggest equality among the parties; the same goes for a round table. Still others prefer no table at all and, instead, like to have the disputants sit in upholstered armchairs around a coffee table or on a comfortable sofa facing the mediator.

6. What the Mediator Knows

At public mediation centers, where mediators work mostly on interpersonal disputes and small consumer claims, the parties usually do not submit any materials before the mediation. The mediator does not meet with the parties individually before meeting with them together, so the session begins with the mediator having little knowledge of the parties other than their names, addresses, and a brief description of the type of dispute they are having.

In other types of mediation (court-connected or with a private mediator), the parties normally will have submitted a short written memorandum to the mediator before the session, stating briefly what the case is about and what they hope to get out of the mediation. In this situation, the mediator already knows something about the dispute and, if necessary, has been able to brush up on the subject—home construction, employment law, or whatever it may be—before the session begins.

E. Stages of the Mediation Session

To understand what happens in mediation, we find it helpful to think of the process as divided into distinct stages. While there are many methods of mediation and lots of energetic discussion in the mediation community about which is best, a very common format is some variation on what's called "interest-based" mediation, and that's the process we'll describe here, leaving the discussion of the relative merits of transformative mediation, narrative mediation, evaluative mediation, and other formats for another book.

Many mediators believe there are six stages of mediation. For mediators who don't caucus, the stages will look slightly different, and of course, there are mediators with entirely different styles for whom these stages won't apply at all. But this is a basic outline of a fairly typical mediation.

I. Stage One: The Mediator's Opening Statement

Often, the mediation session is the first time the parties have seen each other in weeks or months. Now they sit silently across the table, staring at the mediator.

The first lines in this drama are the mediator's and are known as the opening statement. This is a short speech, usually delivered without notes, in which the mediator explains the goals, procedures, and rules of the session. The sample opening remarks that follow next are appropriate for almost any kind of dispute, but the specifics reflect a case involving neighbors, being held at a public mediation center.

Introduce Self and Parties. *Good morning, my name is Peter Lovenheim. I'm the mediator for your case today. Before we go any further, I want to make sure I have everyone's correct name and address. On my left is Rebecca Clarence of 123 Monroe Avenue. Ms. Clarence, you are the claimant in this mediation. And on my right is Arthur Wu, 43 Hilton Place. Mr. Wu, you are the respondent.*

Commend Parties. *I want to commend each of you for choosing mediation as a way to resolve your dispute. Mediating gives you a chance to solve this problem in a cooperative way and with greater flexibility, speed, and privacy than you would likely have in court.*

State Goal. *The Center for Dispute Settlement is a nonprofit organization set up to help people in our community resolve their disputes through mediation. Our goal in this mediation is to help you find a solution to your problem that will be fair to both of you and workable in the long run. Our experience is that disputants who work in good faith during mediation have a very high success rate in reaching an agreement. My job is to help you do that.*

Explain Mediator's Role. *As a mediator, I've been trained and certified by this Center to mediate disputes like this one. I have no authority to make a decision about what will happen. The responsibility for your dispute, and for resolving it, still rests with you.*

I understand from the papers you submitted to start this case that you are neighbors and have some problems about noise, and perhaps some other matters. But beyond that, I have no knowledge of the dispute and no interest in how it is resolved. I am completely neutral. I don't know either of you, and I have no financial, social, or other connections to either of you.

Discuss and Inquire About Timing Issues. *One of the advantages of mediation is that we are under no time pressure. This room is available to us for as long as we want it, and I am prepared to stay here as long as the mediation appears to be productive. If, as we go along, you want to take a break for a cold drink or a stretch, just let me know and we'll do that. Do either of you have any time restrictions that we should discuss?*

Explain Procedure. *We'll begin today by having each of you tell us what this dispute is all about from your point of view. Ms. Clarence, as the claimant, will go first, and then Mr. Wu will have his turn. While one of you is speaking, I'll ask the other person not to interrupt. If you want to make comments later, there are pads and pencils on the table you can use to make notes, and you will also have your chance to speak without interruption. While each of you is speaking, you may notice me taking notes. If I write something, it doesn't mean I agree or disagree with what is being said. I'm taking notes just to help me keep track of the facts of the case.*

Explain the Use of Evidence. *While you are speaking, you can show anything in the way of evidence you have brought with you, such as bills, letters, or photographs. The purpose of evidence is to help us understand your side of the dispute, not to prove who was right and who was wrong. Rules of evidence that apply in a courtroom don't apply here, so any kind of evidence is allowed. The other side will be able to look at it, too. To me, the evidence is less important than what you have to say and how we communicate in the mediation.*

Describe the Discussion Stage. *After opening statements, we'll begin to discuss the issues and hear from any witnesses you have brought. During this discussion phase, you can each say whatever you like, but I will ask you to speak respectfully. That doesn't mean you can't express strong feelings, but only that you need to show respect for the other person and for me—no swearing or other uncivil language.*

Mention Possibility of Caucusing. *At some point I may want to talk with each of you separately in what is called a caucus. If that happens, I will ask one of you to leave the room while I speak with the other. Everything you tell me in a caucus I will keep confidential and not tell the other side, unless you give me specific permission to do so. If I spend longer in caucus with one side than the other, it doesn't mean I am partial to one side; it just means it may be taking me a little longer to understand the facts and options available.*

Stress Confidentiality. *You have both signed an agreement to keep everything said and revealed in this mediation confidential. The Standards of Conduct for Mediators requires that I also keep what you say and show me confidential.*

Describe Consent Agreement. *If we can reach a resolution today, I will help you write it up into an agreement that you will sign and we will have notarized. It will be a binding contract and may be legally enforceable in court. (In disputes involving large sums of money, property, or legal rights, the parties often want a lawyer or business adviser to review an agreement before signing.)*

Invite Questions. *Before we begin with your opening statements, are there any questions? If not, then Ms. Clarence, you are the claimant, so let's begin with you. Please tell us what this case is all about.*

Besides explaining how the mediation session will be conducted, mediators use the opening remarks to help achieve their first and perhaps most important goal: to establish their authority to control the process. They have control at the start, of course, but that is mostly because the parties don't quite know what to expect and are being polite. The first time one side calls the other a liar or a disgrace to the neighborhood, things may quickly get out of hand.

The way mediators keep control as the session moves ahead is by earning the trust, respect, and confidence of the parties. They do this through their statements and their conduct. From the first meeting with the parties, everything the mediator says and does is designed with this goal in mind. When the mediator greets the parties in the waiting area, he or she presents a neat appearance and speaks politely and respectfully. During the opening statement, the mediator speaks confidently, answers the parties' questions fully, and otherwise tries to demonstrate intelligence, knowledge, and neutrality—in short, to show that he or she is someone in whom the parties can and should place their trust.

2. Stage Two: The Parties' Opening Statements

When the mediator is done with opening remarks, the parties are invited to make their own statements. For a disputant (either claimant or respondent), this is a chance, finally and without interruption, to tell the other side and the mediator what the dispute looks like from his or her own point of view.

Consider what an important opportunity this is. Even if a party has tried before the mediation to negotiate a settlement directly with the other side, he or she has probably never had the chance to tell his side of the story without being interrupted or having to shout. Even in court, disputants probably would not get such a chance until the case came to trial and they were called to testify. And then, chances are they would be interrupted by objections from opposing counsel and required to limit their testimony to the narrow legal issues in dispute.

In mediation, the disputant now has the floor. No one will interrupt. No one will object or try to twist his or her words with hostile questions. If the other side interrupts to shout, "That's a lie!" the mediator will intervene and make sure the party gets to finish his or her statement.

While the parties are making their opening statements, they may have the feeling that no one has ever listened to them quite as attentively or with as much understanding as the mediator is listening to them now. This is because mediators use the parties' opening statements not only to learn the facts of the case but also to show they are good listeners. They show that they care about the parties' problems. And not only do they care and understand the problem but they understand the parties' emotional reactions to the problem. This is called *empathic listening*—an important skill that mediators use to help build the parties' trust in them and in the mediation process.

Often, a mediator will go one step further and reflect back to the parties a summary of their opening statements. In essence, the mediator will say, "I heard you say that…" and set out a summary of what each party said, usually right after that party makes their statement. The mediator will then ask, "Have I left anything out or gotten anything wrong?" This gives the party the opportunity to correct misunderstandings or emphasize things that are particularly important to him or her. Summarizing and reflecting back are other helpful tools that build trust between the mediator and the parties at an early stage of the mediation.

3. Stage Three: Discussion

After opening statements by the mediator and the parties, it is time for the parties to start talking directly to each other, with the mediator's active assistance. Often, at the beginning of the discussion stage the mediator will work with the parties to identify the issues that were brought up during the opening statements, and then prioritize them in the order they should best be discussed. A common practice is to tackle the easiest issues first in order to build the disputants' confidence in the mediation process and in their own ability to address their dispute in a reasonable and productive way.

This is also a time for both narrowing and broadening the scope of the mediation. For example, the mediator may try to narrow the number of issues in dispute: Can any complaints discussed in the opening statements be dismissed because they are no longer relevant or were simply based on misinformation? Or, do any issues need to be broadened to include underlying problems, such as hidden interpersonal conflicts, not disclosed by the parties?

Disputants often do not reveal an important issue in their dispute, either because they do not want to or because they honestly do not recognize it themselves. In disputes between business partners, for example, it is often easier for the parties to focus on nuts and bolts business matters like sales, profits, and control than it is to examine underlying personal issues such as career goals, personal financial needs, self-image, and pride. By careful listening and gentle but direct questioning, a skilled mediator can often find clues to underlying issues, even when the parties will not or cannot raise them. It is also during this discussion stage that the parties can question each other and have witnesses speak.

Summarizing and Reflecting Back

The discussion phase is another part of the mediation in which summarizing and reflecting back can be helpful—this time, the parties can do it with each other. After one party speaks, the mediator asks the other party to summarize what that person said. When the second party has finished the summary, the mediator asks the first party whether the summary was accurate and complete. If it wasn't, the first party gets a chance to explain what was missing or misunderstood, and the second party can try again with the summary.

Although this may sound cumbersome, it is actually a very effective way for the parties to feel heard and understood, not just by the mediator but also by the other party. Because each party wants the other person to understand him or her, they are more willing to put genuine effort into understanding the other person. And very often, they discover things they didn't know about how the other person sees the situation and what the other person's real interests are.

4. Stage Four: Caucus

For mediators who use caucusing, the caucus is the guts of the mediation process. Caucusing is a process during which the mediator meets privately with each party one or more times. In caucus, the mediator can talk with a party informally and candidly, and perhaps learn things that the party is reluctant to tell the other side just yet, or offer some insight to the party about their position or interests. In some cases, the caucus is where the business of working out a settlement gets done. In others, the caucus is merely a means of moving things forward so the parties can return to a joint session to hammer out details of a settlement.

The mediator will either ask one side to leave the conference room and wait in the reception area while he or she caucuses with the other side, or have one side move into a second conference room. The mediator will then shuttle back and forth from one room to the other, meeting separately with each side.

When caucusing is used, the mediator typically caucuses with each side several times during the course of a mediation. In a relatively simple two-party case—for example, one involving an auto accident or minor business dispute—it would be typical for a mediator to caucus two or three times with each side during a half-day mediation. A mediation that lasts a full day may involve three to five caucuses with each side. But there is no rule on this. The frequency of caucusing depends entirely on the mediator's style and his or her assessment of whether caucusing is productive.

Confidentiality is essential to the success of caucusing. Usually, the mediator will keep everything said during caucus confidential unless the party clearly states that it may be revealed to the other side. Some mediators do it the other way—they presume that everything said in caucus can be disclosed to the other side unless the party clearly says that it can't be disclosed. In that case, the mediator has to make sure to check before leaving a caucus session about what information needs to be kept confidential.

During caucus, the mediator may probe to find additional facts about the dispute that may reveal underlying issues. What do the parties really want? What is their bottom line? The mediator may be an "agent of reality" and point out weaknesses in one side's positions in order to create doubt and help bring expectations in line with reality. The mediator may also challenge each side to think of new options for settlement and might ask some thought-provoking questions:

- If you were in the other person's shoes, how would you feel?
- What do you think is the strongest part of the other side's position?
- What is the weakest part of your position?
- What will you do if you do not reach an agreement?
- Do you think someone who didn't know you would see you as being entirely without fault in this dispute?
- If this case went to trial, is it realistic to think a jury would find you 100% right and the other side 100% wrong?
- If the other side were to agree to your last proposal, how workable do you think it would be in the long run?
- How much will not reaching an agreement today cost you?
- If this case doesn't settle, how long might it take to get into court?
- If you won in court, could the other side appeal? How long might that leave you in a state of financial uncertainty?
- Can you think of ways to settle this problem that are fair to you and to the other side?
- Are you willing to reach an agreement that works for the other person as well as for you?
- How would it feel to walk away now with this whole matter settled?

Some of the most important questions the mediator asks during caucus are those beginning with "What if?" In other words, the mediator poses the terms of hypothetical settlements: "What if your opponent did X? Would you do Y?"

To Caucus or Not to Caucus

Many mediators do use caucuses as described in this section. However, some feel that mediation can be more productive if everyone stays in the same room the entire time. Most divorce mediators prefer not to caucus, and some mediators who work with business, real estate, and other commercial cases also choose not to use caucuses unless it's absolutely necessary. These mediators tend to have an extremely strong focus on communication, and spend a great deal of time on the discussion phase of the mediation, trying to help the parties understand one another. Most lawyers are more comfortable with the caucus model, so caucusing is more likely if lawyers are present.

5. Stage Five: Joint Negotiations

If caucusing has been successful, the parties at this stage may be focused on a narrower range of issues. They may be looking ahead instead of back, and searching for settlement terms that will satisfy both their own and the other side's real needs. At this point, the mediator may bring both sides back together in the same room to resume joint discussions.

The relationship between disputants often changes at this point. Not only has their negotiation style moved from competitive to more collaborative, but their perceptions of each other are more realistic. Mediator Anne Richan has compared this stage of the mediation to "watching a wall come down brick by brick."

If the parties are able to conduct their own negotiations at this stage, the mediator will take a less active role and listen to be sure that:

- negotiations stay focused on the real issues in dispute
- no new issues emerge that may need to be addressed before negotiations proceed, and
- discussion does not start down a path that may lead to an unworkable settlement (for example, one that would require a party to do something unlawful or impossible to deliver).

The mediator will engage in an exercise called "reality testing," by asking pointed questions about the terms of the settlement in order to make sure it is truly realistic and acceptable to both parties. For example, a mediator might ask a party, "When we began, you said it wouldn't be possible for you to move the location of the fence. Now you've agreed to that—are you sure you'll be able to deliver?"

It is also during this stage that some mediators will intervene, if they think it's necessary, to discourage the parties from settling their dispute on terms that the mediator believes may be unfair to one side. In divorce mediation, for example, when one spouse may be stronger psychologically or have more financial knowledge, most mediators would intervene against an unfair settlement. But in nonfamily disputes, particularly business disputes, most mediators do not see their role as protecting either side. As long as the bargaining has been fair and the settlement terms can realistically be completed, these mediators will allow the parties to reach whatever agreement they believe works for them.

6. Stage Six: Closure

Closure occurs when both sides say yes to the same proposal. Mediation sessions tend to speed up as this point nears; everyone is familiar with the issues, so a kind of shorthand language develops that helps the discussion move to a conclusion. The mediator is more direct in suggesting refinements to possible terms of settlement. The mediator listens carefully to detect the first moment when a package of terms for settlement emerges from negotiations, and tries to recall everything said during the session to be sure no underlying issues threaten the agreement. The mediator also considers whether the settlement strikes a good balance between being specific enough to cover reasonably foreseeable problems but not so overly detailed that it would become too cumbersome to be workable.

When the mediator hears both sides say Okay, it's time to seize the moment.

"Then we have agreement," says the mediator.

Closure.

F. Written Agreements

Where an agreement is reached, it is always a good idea to put some version of it in writing right away, so that the parties can leave with a clear record of what they agreed to do. A written agreement can help make sure that the parties live up to the terms of their settlement.

1. Writing the Agreement

If a case is heard at a public mediation center, typically the mediator will draft the agreement while the parties wait and have them sign it before they leave. Each goes home with a copy. In more complex disputes, where parties may want to have an attorney, accountant, or other adviser review an agreement before signing, the mediator often drafts an outline of the key terms—usually called a memorandum of understanding—for the parties to sign and take with them when they leave.

Typically, the settlement agreement or memorandum of understanding is a short document, written in plain English so everyone can understand it, spelling out what the parties have agreed to do in order to resolve their dispute. It does not say who was at fault for past problems. The agreement is entirely forward-looking, stating in clear terms who has agreed to do what, and when, in order to resolve the matter. If the parties wish, the agreement can be written in the form of a legal contract so that if one side fails to live up to it, the other can sue for breach of contract to have it enforced or be compensated.

How to draft agreements is beyond the scope of this book but is typically covered in mediator training. You can also find some sample settlement agreements in *Mediate, Don't Litigate*, by Peter Lovenheim and Lisa Guerin (Nolo).

Following are examples of two typical settlement agreements, each adapted from actual cases. Identifying information has been altered in order to protect the confidentiality of the parties.

The first agreement concerns a neighborhood dispute heard at a community mediation center. The case involved two families who were next-door neighbors, the Jordons and the Greens. At one time the families, each of which had young children, were friendly, but then tension developed between them. The Jordons complained that Cynthia Green's three children (she is a single mother) often came into their yard uninvited to use their play equipment and left clothes, food wrappers, toys, and other items in the yard. They also complained that Ms. Green's houseguests often parked in a way that blocked their driveway. For her part, Ms. Green complained that the Jordons had made verbal threats against her and her visitors. This agreement was drafted by the two sides with the help of the mediator, and the parties signed the agreement before they left the mediation center.

The Center for Dispute Settlement, Inc.

In the Matter of Mediation Between:

Cynthia Green vs. Daniel and Leslie Jordon

Case Number: C-352–01

Under the Rules and Procedures of The Center for Dispute Settlement, Inc., Cynthia Green and Daniel and Leslie Jordon agree as follows, in order to settle the claims they submitted to Mediation on July 3, 2004.

1. Daniel and Leslie Jordon agree that Ms. Green's children can play on the swing set and other play equipment in the Jordon's backyard at any time they wish as long as they are supervised by an adult.
2. Cynthia Green agrees that she will be responsible for making sure that her children clean up after themselves when they play in the Jordons' yard.
3. Ms. Green agrees that she will be responsible for making sure that her visitors don't park in or block the Jordons' driveway.
4. Mr. and Mrs. Jordon agree not to make any verbal threats to Ms. Green or her visitors, and agree that they will contact her directly in person or by phone if they have any complaints about the conduct of guests at her home.
5. Ms. Green and Mr. and Mrs. Jordon agree that if future disputes arise between them, they will try to resolve them by talking together. If they are unable to do so, they will return to mediation.

If any dispute arises out of this agreement or its performance that Cynthia Green and Daniel and Leslie Jordon cannot resolve themselves, they will try to settle the dispute by mediation through the Center for Dispute Settlement, Inc.

________________	________________	________________
Signature	Signature	Signature
Cynthia Green	Leslie Jordon	(Mediator's name)
	Daniel Jordon	

The next settlement agreement is from a commercial dispute that arose when a large manufacturing company, Abel Corp., claimed machine parts made for it by a smaller firm, ISN, Inc., were defective. Abel Corp. refused further delivery of parts halfway through the contract. ISN claimed the parts conformed perfectly to the specifications in the purchase order and threatened to sue Abel for the actual cost of making the rejected parts. ISN didn't really want to sue, however, because Abel was a major customer—so winning the lawsuit while losing Abel's business would not be in ISN's long-term interest.

The mediation took about four days over a period of three weeks. A brief outline of the agreement's main points was drafted at the final mediation session, then the parties' attorneys worked out the details and prepared a formal agreement. The sample shown is the one that was written at the final mediation session. Note that no one is found at fault. As is typical of settlement agreements, the language is entirely forward-looking in order to help preserve the companies' business relationship to their mutual advantage.

Summary of Mediated Agreement

1. Abel Corp. agrees to award to ISN, Inc., within six months from the signing of a final mediation agreement, a contract or contracts for the manufacture of unspecified machine parts with a net profit margin to ISN upon successful completion of not less than $200,000. Counsel for the parties will draft a document further describing the parties' rights and obligations concerning this agreement for future manufacturing work.
2. Abel will pay to ISN, Inc., not later than 30 days after the signing of a final mediation agreement in this case, the amount of $600,000 to offset part of the costs incurred by ISN, Inc., to manufacture machine parts under the disputed contract that was the subject of this mediation. Full or partial payments of this amount made after the 30-day period will include interest at the rate of 9% per year.
3. As further offset against ISN's manufacturing costs, Abel will purchase from ISN three Model X7 Impurities Testers for a total price of $600,000. Delivery will be made FOB Abel's East Ridge facility within 60 days following the signing of a final mediation agreement. Abel will pay ISN in full for this equipment within 30 days of satisfactory delivery.
4. ISN agrees that when the steps outlined in items 1–3 are completed, it will consider all issues concerning the disputed contract to have been settled and will not in the future bring any legal actions against Abel concerning that contract.
5. The parties will prepare and exchange papers releasing each other from all present legal claims when the steps outlined in items 1–3 are completed.

ISN, INC.

By ______________________________

ABEL CORP.

By ______________________________

____

Mediator

2. If the Parties Don't Reach an Agreement

Although most cases settle in mediation, some do not. Lots of factors can affect the ultimate outcome. If the parties don't reach an agreement, they have several options: they can adjourn the session and agree to come back later and try again; if the case was referred to mediation by a judge, the mediator can send the parties back to court; or if the case has never been to court, one party can sue the other.

One attractive option for parties whose cases do not settle in mediation is arbitration. In arbitration, both sides tell their story to the arbitrator, and the arbitrator makes a decision (see Section A, above, for more about arbitration). In this way, arbitration offers finality; the arbitrator's award is usually legally binding and enforceable by a judge.

Sometimes the parties may want the mediator to "change hats" and arbitrate a decision for them. This poses some problems, particularly if the mediator has received confidential information from the parties during caucus. But it is possible, if the parties agree to it in writing, for a mediator to turn around and arbitrate the same case. The procedure is known as *med-arb*. To avoid conflicts, however, it is more typical for the parties simply to start fresh with a new person acting as a neutral arbitrator.

Now that we've looked at a typical mediation, we'll next discuss the qualities that make a good mediator.

Self-Evaluation: Is Mediation the Right Career for You?

Some trainers estimate that as many as three-quarters of the people who pay for and complete mediator training—a course of study that usually involves 25 to 40 hours in the classroom—never actually practice as mediators. Why? We think it may be because they belatedly discover they are not suited to the work. Some find they are simply not good at mediating; others can mediate well but don't really enjoy it.

There's no particular background required to become a mediator; for the most part, the field remains open to all. But there's no point in investing your time and money in getting trained, only to find you're not suited to the work. This chapter will help you think about whether becoming a mediator is right for you. We'll consider which motivations for wanting to be a mediator make sense and which do not, and what skills and personality traits successful mediators tend to have in common.

The question of what it takes to be a good mediator is tricky. We could list ten personality traits of successful mediators and then discover people who lack every one of them but are excellent at the work nonetheless. Recognizing that this is at best only a rough answer to a tough question, here are some thoughts on the personal qualities that tend to make someone a successful mediator.

A. Motivations to Mediate

People have many different reasons for wanting to become mediators. Some of these are based on a practical understanding of the field, while others may be based more on wishful thinking than reality. How do these various motivations tend to play out once people begin practicing? Let's consider some of the reasons people have for entering this field—some sensible, some less so.

1. To Be of Service

Ours has been called a litigious society. We have more than a million lawyers and file more lawsuits per person than any other nation in the world. When we experience disappointment or are in conflict, our conditioned battle cry is, "See you in court!" As one observer noted, "We call our lawyers to sue before we call our opponents to talk." Some of the lawsuits people bring might be amusing if they weren't such obvious examples of litigation overkill, like the group of parents who sued all the way to federal court over an official's error in a high school football game, or the man who sued a restaurant because his pat of butter weighed less than two full ounces.

Although mediation is not a cure-all, it can help resolve many of our interpersonal and commercial disputes without litigation, saving people from wasting time and money, freeing them from lawyers, and helping them solve their problems without destroying their important personal, family, and business relationships.

We need more people to help transform our society from one of aggressive conflict to one of cooperative problem solving. We need those people who can, to help others work out solutions to their own problems quickly, fairly, and inexpensively so they can get on with their lives. To be a part of this historic transformation is a worthy reason to become a mediator and a motivation that will sustain you through both the uplifting and the frustrating parts of the work.

On a more direct human level, being a mediator gives you the opportunity to help relieve immediate suffering on a daily basis. Nearly everyone who comes to mediation does so because they are in conflict and want to end it, or because they are enduring a painful transition, such as a divorce or the end of a long business relationship. In many cases the conflict or transition is causing significant disruption in their lives, often creating lots of emotional upheaval.

Although the mediation process can be hard work for everyone involved, the end result can bring enormous relief. For a mediator, there are few pleasures as gratifying as meeting two disagreeing disputants at nine o'clock in the morning and by mid-afternoon watching them shake hands and leave with a signed agreement. The satisfaction of knowing you've helped people close out a painful chapter of their lives in a way that feels comfortable to them, and the visible relief you can see on their faces when they complete an agreement, can make you feel that you are truly being of service.

Case Study

Father and Son

A recent case of Peter's involved a father and 27-year-old son who had been estranged for many years. The son said the father cared little for him and was too busy for him. The father said it was impossible to talk with his son because he would blow up at the most innocent remark. They met with the mediator for four hours over two late afternoon sessions. They worked hard, each owned up to his own part in the dispute, and together they reached deeply to find solutions.

At the end of the second session, they worked together to come up with the terms of an agreement: regular family dinners, weekly meetings for coffee, use of civil language, respect for each other's work, and so on. Peter read the agreement aloud and each person signed it. As they put on their coats to leave, the son turned to his father and said, "I really do love you, Dad," and the father said, "I love you, too, son." They embraced, and left together.

This is mediation at its best and most rewarding.

2. To Do Work That Is Meaningful and Enjoyable

Mediators get an intimate view into people's lives. Whether you're mediating a divorce, a business case with underlying personal issues, or a personal injury matter in which a person's ability to navigate life is in question, it can be both stimulating and profoundly satisfying to be involved so closely with real people and their problems. Many find they enjoy this close-up view of others' lives and challenges and find great satisfaction in supporting others as they solve life-altering problems.

For most mediators, the process itself is enjoyable despite its frequent frustrations. A well-timed or well-crafted question from the mediator can sometimes change the entire tone of the mediation—and often, the parties themselves will find ways of using the process to shift, compromise, and sometimes be more generous than anyone in the room imagined was possible at the beginning. Any mediator can tell you that mediation is not magic—it involves a lot of hard work by everyone involved—but there are moments when it seems to be.

Not all cases end well, of course. Some sputter along, accomplishing little; some end without an agreement. But even in these, one can enjoy working with people as they try hard to resolve difficult problems. Even if it's just one of them working hard, or even if its just one of them working hard part of the time, there can still be pleasure in it for the mediator. And even when it's frustrating, it can also be fascinating.

3. To Make a Good Living

If you think you can derive this kind of enjoyment from helping people move through the mediation process—whatever the results—you have a good reason to become a mediator. If you think you're going to get enormously wealthy doing it, you'd better think again.

Twenty years ago, about the only people making a living at mediation were a few hot-shot business mediators flying around the country resolving multi-million-dollar construction disputes. But that has changed: mediation is more accepted; it is even sought-after today. Very well-known mediators working with the largest mediation services like JAMS and AAA (described in detail in Chapter 5) earn a percentage of what the agency charges for their time, which can be many hundreds of dollars per hour. Likewise private practitioners at prestigious mediation firms like Gregorio, Haldeman & Piazza in San Francisco charge substantial sums (Tony Piazza commands fees of up to $10,000 per day).

These folks aside, however, few of us actually get rich. As noted, most mediators charge by the hour. At $100 to $150 an hour you can earn a good living, but you aren't going to become wealthy; there are just not enough hours in a day. And don't think you'll get wealthy mediating huge, multi-million-dollar business disputes and taking a cut—it's against mediator ethics to charge based on the outcome of a case (see Appendix B for standards of conduct for mediators).

Still, it's entirely possible to make a decent living as a mediator, and many people are doing it. Mediators are doing well with divorce mediation, civil disputes, business cases, and environmental matters. Still others teach and train or work in human resource offices of large corporations, universities, and other institutions. Add to that another set of jobs in what we call mediation support: people who administer private dispute resolution companies or government programs, sell the services of private firms, operate Internet mediation services, and train other mediators. And there are mediation-related jobs that use many of the same skills you learn as a mediator, like ombuds work, training, coaching, and facilitation. We'll discuss all of these options in more detail in Chapters 5, 6, and 7.

In sum, if you're thinking of becoming a mediator to become wealthy, you're likely to be disappointed. But if you are satisfied making a reasonable salary and care more about the other benefits of the career, read on.

4. To Solve Other People's Problems by Telling Them What to Do

Some people like to solve other people's problems. You probably know the type. At the office they are always willing to close the door and listen to someone else's personal or business dilemma. But they don't stop with just listening; they go the next step and tell the troubled person exactly what to do and how to do it. Sometimes they want a full report later about how their advice worked out. It's good to have people like this around; they can be very helpful. The only problem is, except for the listening part, it's not what mediators do.

Good mediators overcome the temptation to solve the parties' problem by telling them what they should do, and instead are content to support the parties' efforts to solve their problem themselves. More often than not, people who become mediators because they like to solve others' problems are surprised to see how resistant the parties are when they try to impose solutions.

Some people are drawn to mediation for the challenge of getting disputants to make an agreement. We see this most often with other professionals—notably lawyers—who are used to achieving positive outcomes for their clients. They just love the challenge of charging right into a conflict and getting results! But sometimes the more the mediator emphasizes results, the more resistant the parties become. Seasoned mediators know that often it's only by letting go of concern for results that they can get them. It's a paradox, but it's true. Sometimes it's only when the mediator can say, "Folks, it's really okay with me if you choose not to reach an agreement," that the parties become willing to take ownership of the dispute and get serious about settling.

So if you're thinking of becoming a mediator so you can tell everyone else how to solve their problems or because you love the challenge of getting results, think again.

CAUTION: Mediating Can Sometimes Be Lonely, Stressful, and Emotionally Draining

It's very common for mediators to hear "I'd love to have that job!" from others who are tired of putting up with the stress of law practice, business, academia—whatever it is they're currently doing. Most mediators love their jobs. But that doesn't mean it's easy all the time.

It can, of course, be a tremendous ego trip to sit down with people and help them work out their problems. It can be uplifting, a natural high, a great source of satisfaction. You can go home at the end of the day feeling you've really accomplished something. But mediators do pay a price. Labor mediator and professor Jerome T. Barrett, in his paper "The Psychology of a Mediator," identifies aspects of mediating that can exact a psychic cost:

Isolation: most of the mediator's work is alone, without colleagues and supervisors.

Helper Role: the mediator's power is limited to that of a helper; without the will of the disputing parties, the mediator is powerless to make things happen.

Limited Positive Feedback: the very human needs of the mediator for recognition, appreciation, and respect are generally unfulfilled by the parties, as they focus—appropriately—on their own disputes.

Confidential Information: the absolute requirement of confidentiality places on the mediator the same pressures that a priest has regarding confession and a lawyer has with a client.

Filtered Reaction Role: to maintain their impartial role and retain their effectiveness, mediators must suppress such normal reactions as frustration, hostility, and anger and replace them by neutral or opposite reactions.

In summary, observes Barrett,

"[the mediator is] an outside intervenor, working under high stress on the problems of others . . . in isolation from any support groups, and bound by a strict code of confidentiality. The mediator's opportunities for positive feedback are limited, the success of his performance is difficult to measure, and he is subjected to the manipulations of the parties."

Yet "in spite of the psychic costs," concludes Barrett, "there is no shortage of candidates for the job, and incumbents talk glowingly about a 'high' from achieving a difficult settlement."

Source: Jerome T. Barrett, "The Psychology of a Mediator," Society for Professionals in Dispute Resolution (now ACR), Washington, DC 1983, Occasional Paper No. 83-1.

B. Skills and Personality Traits of Successful Mediators

Assuming one enters the field for the right reasons, are there particular skills or personality traits likely to make one a successful mediator? Most mediators would probably agree that some skills and traits are common among those who succeed in this field. The skills can often be learned, while the personality traits discussed here are generally innate.

Nevertheless, most mediators would acknowledge that someone with very different skills and traits could also make a good mediator. Michael Lang, a seasoned mediator and trainer, expressed this well when asked about mediator personalities. He wrote:

"I am asked this question often in trainings, particularly because many of the participants experience me as having a personality that is well-suited to the work (calm, able to tolerate ambiguity, respectful, empowering, etc.). At the same time, I know many mediators whose personalities differ vastly from mine and whom I regard as superior mediators."

With that as a disclaimer, we offer the following very general guidelines that may help you assess your suitability for the field.

1. Good Listening Skills

Chapter 1 referred to the crucial role that listening skills play in the mediator's ability to understand what a dispute is about and to earn the participants' trust. We label this kind of listening "empathic", as it involves listening not only to the facts but also to the emotions behind them. It is really very different from the kind of listening we generally do on a day-to-day basis. Mediators must listen with their full attention, focusing completely on the party who is speaking while still attending to the process as a whole.

"Once participants have had the experience of being heard fully by the mediator," observes Jim Melamed, "they are willing to turn over leadership of the mediation to the mediator; but before they have had that experience, they will resist the mediator's lead."

Mediator training devotes a great deal of time to the theory of good listening, as well as to role playing to practice specific techniques. So although good listening comes naturally to some people, others can develop the skill through study and practice.

So You Think You're a Good Listener?

Some people are naturally good listeners, and even more of us believe we are listening effectively when in reality, we may not be doing the greatest job of it. For example, when you are listening to someone else, are you busy developing your rebuttal to what they are saying? Even if you agree with them, are you thinking about what you want to say, and waiting for your opening? Are you evaluating and judging everything they say? Do you assume that you know what they are going to say next? These are very common ways of listening that can impede really good communication. It's important that you make an honest evaluation of yourself to see if you tend to be distracted in any of these ways.

On the other hand, certain ways of listening will enhance communication and make the speaker feel listened to. Do you make eye contact while you are engaged in conversation? Do you nod and make noises that show you are being attentive? Is your body language open and friendly? All of these things will help your listener to feel heard.

If you want to learn more about listening and improve your listening skills, there are dozens of books on the subject, and a great deal of information available on the Web. You can find some of these resources at www.listen.org, the website of the International Listening Association.

Listening is one of the most important skills that a mediator uses, and there are very few of us who couldn't improve our skills, so make sure you take seriously your learning in this area.

2. Ability to "Read" People

When we're mediating, parties give us information about the dispute during their opening statements, in joint discussions, and in private caucus if we are caucusing. Even so, the parties seldom tell us everything we need to know about the dispute, their reactions to it, and their willingness to consider various options for settlement. Indeed, throughout the session, unexpressed interests, needs, and emotions float about the room. Therefore, the ability to read the parties—a largely intuitive ability to sense the things we are not being told, to perceive emotions that linger just below the surface, and to push with questions a bit further in a particular direction—can go a long way toward making one successful as a mediator.

Sensing a party's dissatisfaction with the process, for example, can allow a mediator to surface issues that otherwise might have been in the way of the parties reaching a settlement. And at the other end of the spectrum, being tuned in to when a party responds nonverbally to a statement, or even a proposal, can give the mediator clues about what terms of settlement might be acceptable.

The ability to read other people seems to be innate in some people, while others seem to develop it as they go through life. Others may never develop an intuitive sense, but at the very least, most people can learn some basic information—like how to interpret body language—to try to improve their intuitive grasp of a situation.

3. Facility With Language

Like psychological counseling and therapy, mediation is a "talking cure." The entire process, from opening statements to writing up the final agreement, involves words. Accordingly, a facility—indeed, a precision—with language contributes greatly to being a successful mediator.

Throughout the session, the mediator must repeatedly capture and echo back in a few precise words the sometimes puzzling stories and complicated expressions of the parties, and help the parties express their often vaguely understood goals in clear and simple terms. Mediators who fire off words casually may quickly find themselves in trouble, perhaps having said things that weren't as clear or as neutral, respectful, or caring as they should have been.

A mediator's facility with language also becomes crucial as the parties near agreement. The mediator must convey proposals, and the reasons behind those proposals, from each side to the other, with complete accuracy. Once an agreement has been reached, the mediator must be able to state the parties' agreements accurately in terms that both parties fully understand and that reflect what was actually agreed, so that the agreement can be reality-tested and closure can be reached.

Mediators also need good language skills to draft written agreements. In larger cases, you may just outline the terms and instruct the parties to take it to their lawyers, accountants, or other advisers for review. Even there, you will need to be clear, concise, and accurate. And in smaller cases, you'll actually draft the agreement, and careful use of language is essential. You'll need to express exactly and completely what the parties have agreed to, in plain English, without any mention of fault or blame. The writing must be concise enough so the document stays reasonably short and understandable, but it has to contain enough detail so its meaning is clear to the parties not only today—after they've just spent three hours discussing the issues in detail—but three years from now, when they refer to it long after their memories of the discussion have faded.

For these reasons, most successful mediators are people who like words and are comfortable expressing themselves verbally. Still, these essential skills can be learned by anyone who has basic language abilities, through mediator training as well as classes in clear writing.

4. A Calm Demeanor

Parties in mediation are under stress. They are, after all, sitting across the table from the person or persons whom they see as the source of their problem. The mediator, therefore, needs to be able to project a sense of calm to help them feel safe and relaxed enough to participate in the mediation. As Jim Melamed puts it, some people have their idle set very high. There is a certain frenetic pace to how they conduct themselves, and generally, those people are not going to end up as the best mediators. Mediation requires you to create a certain contemplative environment, with the discussion often moving at the rate of the slowest participant.

At the same time, some excellent and much sought-after mediators do have a very high idle. And the mediator cannot be too laid-back without draining all the energy out of the session. So there is really no hard and fast rule about temperament. In most cases, though, a calm but purposeful demeanor seems to work best.

Related to a calm personality is, as mediator Michael Lang pointed out earlier, an ability to accept ambiguity. A good mediator must be comfortable discussing, sometimes for hours, a situation in which it will never be established who did what to whom or who was right and who was wrong. And during negotiations, several very different avenues toward possible settlement will often remain open and under discussion simultaneously. One has to be comfortable dealing with this kind of uncertainty. If you get ruffled by it, are easily put on edge, or need things to be very controlled and controllable, your discomfort may affect the parties and undercut the chances for a successful outcome.

5. Ability to Understand Complex Facts

A mediator needs to be able to understand complicated fact patterns, so a reasonable degree of abstract reasoning ability and intelligence is necessary. And you do need to be able to grasp the general picture of what is going on pretty quickly.

However, mediation is not a debating society where you're trying to outsmart the other people in the room, and you can slow down the session to give yourself time to consider the details of what you've heard and process the information. You can do this by letting the parties talk about tangential subjects while you digest what you've heard; you can take a break before and after going into caucus; or you can simply say you need to call a recess to consider what you've heard and then schedule another session for the following week. You can also ask the parties to help you process information by asking them what they consider to be the most important elements of their conflict, or how they see the situation.

Because there are so many ways to slow the process down and bring yourself up to speed, you needn't despair of being a mediator if you think you are a slow study. But make sure that you feel comfortable digesting and discussing a lot of facts at one time, and that you think you can at least do that quickly enough to keep a session on track.

6. Trustworthiness in Keeping Confidences

Keeping confidences is the currency of a good mediator, and no one who doesn't have that ability should be mediating. Keeping confidences may sound easy if you haven't been put to the test. But mediators face this challenge both inside and outside the mediation room. Inside the session, the mediator is meeting in private caucus with each party and receiving sensitive information that must be held confidential from the other side unless the party who told it gives permission. After one or two rounds of caucuses, knocking around in the mediator's head is a fairly complex list of things revealed by both sides, some of which the mediator may have permission to reveal but much of which must be kept secret. Keeping all that straight while in the midst of conducting negotiations toward a settlement is no easy task.

But even tougher sometimes is protecting the confidence of your clients outside the session—protecting it absolutely. That means not even revealing who the participants in a case were. It's possible that you may be called upon to mediate sensitive personal matters with people well known to you and to others in your family. Even then, you would be prohibited from revealing to anyone, even your spouse or partner, that you had even met with these people.

In this regard, the mediator carries the same burdens of confidentiality that a therapist, lawyer, or clergyperson does. And in the unlikely event you are called to testify in a court of law or arbitration proceeding and asked to reveal information about what was said in the mediation session, your clients and the entire profession of mediation will be relying on you to refuse to breach that oath of confidentiality, regardless of what the personal cost to you might be. Think carefully about whether this is a professional burden you are willing to undertake. If you are someone who likes to gossip or who thinks that even when you promise to keep a secret, it's okay to tell your spouse because "pillow talk" is excepted, mediation is probably not a good career for you.

7. Professional Detachment

As a mediator, you will be privy to an intimate look into the lives of your clients. You will see their pain, dashed hopes, life-transforming injuries, wrecked marriages, and ruined businesses. You help them through the mediation process and hope that it relieves some of their suffering. But ultimately, you can't change their lives. And once the mediation is over, you are powerless to do more. They are unlikely ever to talk with you about the matter again.

Some people are good at maintaining a professional detachment from their clients' lives so that once a session is over, they close the file and move on to the next case. Other people are unable to do this; they get too wrapped up in the lives of their clients and just cannot let go. They feel an overwhelming temptation to follow up, to try to be of further help, even just to find out what happened next. While a small amount of follow-up is sometimes appropriate, in general you will need to have very clear boundaries and keep your own emotional needs for closure separate from the needs of the parties.

No mediator succeeds all the time. One of the frustrations of being a mediator is that one has no control over the facts in dispute or the attitudes of the disputants. Some cases, due to especially thorny issues or especially thorny people, just cannot be successfully mediated, even with the finest mediator doing a first-rate job. In such cases, the good mediator will end the mediation without a settlement and accept the result without seeing it as a personal failing.

If you are, by nature, too sensitive to let go and detach from clients' lives, or if you need cases to come out "right" in your own view, then mediation may not be for you. It could be too painful, and ultimately you might get yourself into trouble for violating professional ethics.

8. Sense of Humor and Sense of Drama

Mediators often use humor to relieve tension during a session. Telling a joke or a humorous story at the appropriate time can be a good way to distract the parties when they get off track or when anxiety is so high they cannot continue with a rational discussion. But humor can also backfire or be offensive if it's not done well, so having a sense for the appropriateness and timing of humor is important.

A related skill is what we could call a sense of the drama in mediation. A mediation session has a setting: the conference room, the table and chairs, the blank pads of paper. And there's a cast of characters: you, the disputants, their supporters or friends. And then there's a plot: the six-stage process leading, ideally, to a resolution. The opening lines of the drama—the mediator's opening statement—are yours, but thereafter you must lead the parties through this dramatic encounter. The skill with which you do this depends in part on your sense of the drama inherent in the process. As the "director," you must decide, for example, how much to allow the tension to build before defusing it with a distracting joke or story, how hard to push during caucus to move a party off an initial demand, how to present a new idea for settlement, and, in the later stages, when to cue the parties that a shift in negotiating position would be helpful.

In many of us a sense of humor is inborn, and it's hard to develop as an adult, though perhaps not impossible. Likewise, although some of the sense of the drama of mediation can be learned in training, much of it, like the ability to read participants, is innate. It may take some practice before you know whether you have these qualities—at least in the context of a mediation session. If you do mediate, try to be as honest as possible in your self-assessment.

9. Patience, Perseverance, and Optimism

More than many professions, mediation truly requires patience and perseverance. No matter how good you are at the job and how hard you work, there are always at least two other people in the room whose attitudes, actions, and words you cannot control. You may come to see a clear path toward resolution of the parties' dispute after just an hour of mediation, while the parties continue to struggle just to communicate. Maybe they will reach the same solution you thought of, and maybe they will come up with another. In the meantime, you have to persevere in your efforts, patiently and calmly.

Your patience may be most often taxed during the middle and later stages of a session, when the parties may insist on raising lots of seemingly minor issues, all of which have to be laboriously worked through before you can get them to focus on the major one and resolve it. Often there comes a time when whatever goodwill the parties came in with or developed seems to have disappeared, and one or even both of them threaten to leave.

Another testing point often comes toward the end of the session when the parties have reached a settlement in principle but insist on repeated changes in the wording of the agreement. It's been reported, for example, that to satisfy Israeli and Egyptian negotiators, President Carter and his mediation team at Camp David drafted no fewer than 23 versions of a proposed peace agreement. In his diary, Carter wrote, "I resolve to do everything possible to get out of the negotiating business." Fortunately, President Carter persevered in his work as a mediator, and since he left office has helped settle many international disputes. Still, the frustration he expressed is something with which many mediators can identify and something those thinking of entering the field should consider.

A sense of optimism is also important. If you are constantly thinking that things aren't going well, you will probably convey that attitude to the parties without meaning to. Sometimes, the mediator's simple statement "I'm not discouraged" can give the parties renewed energy for working toward a resolution. If you are by nature a rather negative person, mediation might not be a good career option for you. On the other hand, if you have a generally positive outlook—or are willing to try to develop one—you will have a great tool at your disposal.

10. Self-Marketing and Political Skills

Some people pay for and successfully complete mediator training, rent an office, buy furniture and equipment, take a listing in the yellow pages, and then sit back waiting for the phone to ring. After a year, they may still not have mediated a single case. They are among the naive victims of a common delusion: that lots of people are just waiting to come to a mediator to settle their disputes.

It's true, of course, that loads of disputes could be settled by a mediator. The problem is that most people never think of picking up the phone and calling one. Though it is continuing to grow by leaps and bounds, mediation is still too new for that. So until such time as mediators are as popular as lawyers, successful mediators will need an entrepreneurial spirit. If you want the phone to ring, you're going to have to get out there and market your services to the people who can be your clients or who can refer clients to you.

Some people have the personality for doing this; they like meeting people and are natural self-promoters. Others shy away from these activities; for them, the process is painful and often unsuccessful. Yet the reality of the marketplace, especially private practice, requires a lot of self-promotion.

For example, if you are considering a private practice in family and divorce mediation, you'll need to send letters of introduction to people who can refer cases to you—therapists, clergy, and lawyers. Then you'll need to follow up with phone calls, meetings, and lunches, and arrange opportunities to speak about mediation to groups at community centers, churches, and social clubs. If your interest lies more in business mediation, you'll need to go through the same process with people such as business owners, accountants, consultants, lawyers, and officials from the chamber of commerce.

Private practice also requires good political skills, such as the ability to make and maintain long-term business contacts, to scope out the competition, and to maintain comfortable relations with other mediators in your community, even when you are in direct competition. This shouldn't be hard, as mediators are a collegial bunch, but you must do your part.

Political skills are also essential if you're planning to work within an institution—a court system, school, or large business. To understand how the institution works and how to navigate layers of management, you'll need good political instincts. Your survival and professional growth within the organization will depend on it. We'll talk more about these aspects of mediation practice in Chapters 6 and 7, but it's worth keeping in mind that if you don't have the ability or desire to sell yourself, private practice is probably not for you. And in any type of practice, good political skills are essential.

Mediator Skills and Personality Traits: At a Glance

- Good Listening Skills
- Ability to "Read" People
- Facility With Language
- A Calm Demeanor
- Ability to Understand Complex Facts
- Trustworthiness in Keeping Confidences
- Professional Detachment
- Sense of Humor and Sense of Drama
- Patience, Perseverance, and Optimism
- Self-Marketing and Political Skills

C. Conclusion

We've attempted to identify some of the personality traits and skills common to successful mediators. Some of these you can learn in a good training program. Others tend to be innate; some people have them and others do not. Yet as we emphasized earlier, some mediators lack many of these traits but have other abilities—call them intuitive peacemaking skills—that nevertheless allow them to succeed as mediators. Mediation trainers have seen it over and over again—someone comes in who doesn't fit the profile, doesn't seem to learn the skills very well, isn't naturally humorous or quick to grasp people or situations. Nonetheless, the person goes on to work at a nonprofit mediation center and to help settle cases—using qualities other than those we've described.

So use the above list as best you can to evaluate yourself as a potential mediator, but bear in mind that no list is definitive. The only way to know for sure whether you would be a good mediator and enjoy the work is to get some basic training and try your hand at a few cases. In the next chapter, we'll look at different kinds of training programs and how you can select training that is best suited to your needs. ●

Where Mediators Work

The field of mediation is vast and varied. In this chapter, we have divided into six very broad categories the most common places where mediators work: (1) community mediation centers, (2) court-connected programs, (3) government programs, (4) private dispute resolution companies, (5) private practice, and (6) corporate, association, and specialty programs. We'll describe the kinds of cases handled in each type of program, and the backgrounds of the mediators who work there.

With an understanding of these various types of services, you'll have a broad overview of what the mediation field looks like today. Where you might fit in as a mediator will depend on your skills and career goals, as well as the mediation services available in your community.

Six Types of Mediation Service at a Glance

Mediation Service	Case Types	Mediator Background
Community mediation center	Interpersonal, small claims, landlord-tenant, neighborhood	Varied, no professional background needed
Court-connected program	Contract disputes, personal injuries, divorce, minor criminal complaints	Law, social work, criminal justice, psychology
Government program	Employment discrimination and wrongful termination, taxation, securities	Law, labor relations, securities, human resources
Private dispute resolution companies	Business contracts, personal injuries, construction, employment	Law, business, human resources, accounting, psychology
Independent mediators: Divorce	Divorce and family	Social work, law, psychology, parenting
Independent mediators: Specialty and general	Business, construction, personal injury	Law, business, construction, accounting, insurance
Corporate, association, and specialty programs	Employment, real estate, interpersonal, ethnic and religious discrimination	Human resources, social work, business, religious or ethnic background

A. Community Mediation Centers

Public mediation centers, also called community mediation centers, fill an important need for low-cost mediation services at the local level. The federal government has never provided much funding for mediation centers, despite the success rate demonstrated in studies of mediation programs. Fortunately, state and local governments have stepped in to fill the gap. In 1975, there were fewer than a dozen public mediation centers around the country; today, nearly 600 centers serve U.S. communities from coast to coast, handling tens of thousands of cases per year.

Community mediation centers are usually nonprofit organizations that receive funds from state and local governments to provide low-cost mediation services to the public. They are called by various names, such as Dispute Resolution Center, Neighborhood Justice Center, Community Boards, and Center for Dispute Settlement.

Community mediation centers truly live up to their name. The center staff, mediators, parties, and issues are all based in the local community, and the community reaps tremendous benefits from the centers' work. As we'll discuss in later chapters, these centers are great resources for new mediators looking for training and experience. And many experienced mediators continue volunteering at community mediation centers even after they have an established practice, because the work can be enormously satisfying.

1. Types of Cases That Community Mediation Centers Handle

In the early years of community mediation, nonprofit centers had the reputation of handling mostly what are sometimes referred to as "park-and-bark" cases—neighborhood disputes involving pets, noise, kids, shared driveways, and the like. Whether or not park-and-bark was ever a fair description of the early centers' caseloads, today most centers handle a mix of neighborhood, consumer, small business, assault, harassment, victim-offender reconciliation, and family and roommate disputes. Services at public mediation centers are available to all local residents and generally are provided free, on a sliding scale, or at nominal set cost (perhaps $10 to $25 per party).

The great strength of community mediation centers is that they are a cost-effective way of resolving minor cases that often get lost in, or otherwise are not well served by, local courts and the criminal justice system. Judges, police, district attorneys, and social service agencies often refer cases to community mediation centers. Charges of assault without injury, personal harassment, and disputes between spouses are typical of cases that might be referred. The centers also handle disputes brought to them directly by the people involved; these problems might include noise from late-night parties, claims of harassment between ex-spouses and partners, employment problems, and consumer small claims, such as those involving dry cleaning or auto repair.

Some centers have also developed special programs to meet specific local needs. For example, centers in college towns may hear lots of disputes between roommates, and centers in rural areas may hear disputes between farmers and feed companies or bankers, or between mobile home park owners and tenants.

Community mediation can also sometimes handle major community disputes, such as where an entire neighborhood is in conflict with a developer who wants to build a structure the neighbors find offensive. These are especially interesting cases to work on if you are a volunteer for a nonprofit center. But as you can see, you have lots of opportunities to learn how to mediate a variety of disputes (and contribute to your community) when you volunteer at a community mediation center.

How to find a local community mediation center. To find out whether there is a center in your community where you could get trained and/or volunteer, check the yellow pages under "mediation," or try the general information number at city hall or the local bar association. If this doesn't produce results, check the website for the National Association for Community Mediation, an organization that represents more than half of the community mediation centers in the country, at www.nafcm.org. You'll find contact information for nearly 300 centers nationwide.

---

2. Mediators at Community Mediation Centers

Trained volunteers handle most cases at community mediation centers. Some centers pay mediators a small stipend, maybe $25 or $50 a case. But the bulk of the work is done on a volunteer basis.

Volunteer mediators at nonprofit centers come from a variety of professional and work backgrounds: teaching, social work, law, business, parenting and homemaking, and journalism, among others. Many professional mediators volunteer their time at community centers even after they have established mediation practices, but the majority of volunteers are community members who have other day jobs or are retired.

Most of the state laws that establish community mediation centers set minimum standards for training. A typical program would involve about 25 classroom hours plus a supervised period of apprenticeship.

The following profile is representative of a typical mediator working as a volunteer at a community mediation center. (This and all other mediator profiles in the book use mediators' real names, are based on interviews, and are used with permission.)

MEDIATOR PROFILE

Name: Joan Chisholm

Title: Volunteer mediator

Mediation Service: Community Dispute Settlement Program, Media, Pennsylvania

Educational Background: Master's degree in education with postgraduate work

Years in Practice: 12

Professional Affiliations: African-American Alliance of Peacemakers

Number of Cases Handled in Career: hundreds

Current Caseload: One or two a month (Joan also works as a compensated mediator with the U.S. Postal Service)

Case Types: Custody of children of separated and divorced parents; neighborhood disagreements such as shared driveways; disputes about neighbors' children, noise, older neighbors, harassment, and other cases referred by local courts

Most Memorable Mediation Moment: "The parties refused to be in the same room together, so my co-mediator and I had to shuttle back and forth between two rooms. After an hour and a half, the co-mediator convinced them it would be better if they sat down in the same room and faced each other. When they agreed to do that, it felt terrific."

Notable Features of My Conference Room: "I mediate where the parties are—at churches, schools, day care centers."

Philosophy of Mediation: "I try to help people see there is a better path they can take that is nonthreatening and full of promise."

B. Court-Connected Mediation Programs

Many state—and even some federal—courts have initiated mediation programs as a way to reduce their caseloads and operating costs. Typically under these programs, people who file lawsuits are required or strongly encouraged to try mediation before they are allowed to proceed with their case.

States with broad court-referral programs include California, Florida, Georgia, Minnesota, Michigan, New Hampshire, Texas, and Utah, but nearly every state today has some kind of program available. Some states require that parties receive a written notice about the availability of mediation but do not require them to pursue it.

In some states, the court itself provides the parties with conference rooms and mediators. In others, judges or court clerks simply instruct the parties to pick a mediator from a list of qualified mediators or to go out and find their own mediator. The cost of court-connected mediation to the parties varies from state to state and program to program. In some courts you are required to pay a fee for mediation services, and in others the court provides services at no cost.

1. Types of Cases That Court-Connected Mediation Programs Handle

Court-connected mediation programs handle nearly the entire range of cases that find their way through the courthouse doors. Most programs handle civil (noncriminal) cases such as contract disputes, personal injury claims, employment, and civil rights cases. Family court programs handle divorce and family issues, and victim-offender and restorative justice programs deal with criminal complaints. Many small claims courts also have mediation programs, either voluntary or mandatory.

2. Mediators in Court-Connected Programs

Many of the mediators working in court-connected programs are lawyers. In family court programs, discussed in Section 4, below, mediators often are social workers or therapists. Some work full time for the court, and others work on a contract basis. Mediators who work in or with the criminal courts, in victim-offender reconciliation or restorative justice programs, come from more varied backgrounds and often are laypeople—in fact, some of these programs provide most of their mediation services through community mediation centers, using primarily volunteers.

3. Federal Court Programs

Federal law requires all federal district courts to authorize the use of alternative dispute resolution (ADR) in civil cases, and to require that litigants consider using some form of ADR. In many districts, the court gives parties a choice of what type of ADR they want to use, including mediation; in others, mediation is the only option offered.

The courts are also required to establish qualifications for their neutrals, including mediators, but the courts have a lot of discretion in setting those standards. However, it would be very unusual to find a federal district court that would be willing to use nonlawyers as mediators for federal lawsuits.

Most federal court programs don't hire mediators to work exclusively for the court, but have a panel of private practice lawyer-mediators with extensive experience in federal litigation. The program provides mediation training and then refers cases according to the each mediator's area of expertise.

4. State Court and Local Programs

State court mediation programs vary enormously in their procedures and in how they use and compensate mediators. In some states, local trial courts operate their own mediation programs, and assign a mediator to cases at an early stage. In others, local bar associations operate mediator referral programs on behalf of the courts, and litigants can choose from a list of mediators maintained by the bar association. The level of training required of the mediators, and the degree of screening done by the court or bar association, also varies widely. Mediators may be court employees, volunteers, or paid outside contractors.

For a state-by-state summary of court-connected mediation programs, see the website of the National Center for State Courts (www.ncsconline.org) and follow the site map to the alternative dispute resolution section and the mediation subsection, where an NCSC document provides links to the court-connected programs of every state. You can also find information on court-connected ADR at the website of the Center for Analysis of Alternative Dispute Resolution Systems (CAADRS) at www.caadrs.org. Finally, Appendix D lists statewide mediation programs, which would be a useful resource in your state for finding local court-connected mediation programs.

a. Divorce Mediation Programs

Most U.S. states have a special type of court-connected mediation to handle divorce cases. Some states simply refer couples to private mediation services, but in many states (for example, California), the courts themselves operate extensive mediation programs for divorcing couples. In most of these programs, the mediation is limited to parenting issues such as child custody and visitation. In a few states, couples can mediate financial issues (such as division of property) through court programs; in others, they may have to undertake a separate, private mediation to deal with those issues.

Court-connected divorce mediation may be provided free or at nominal cost, or parties might have to pay market rate. Typically, the mediation lasts just one or two sessions, because the court often requires the mediation be limited to parenting issues and because the volume of cases is high and staff resources are stretched thin.

Mediators in some family court programs are required by law to protect the interests of the children—to raise questions about the children's welfare (even if the child's parents do not) and even to block an agreement if it does not adequately protect the children's interests. In some states, mediators have the power to make a recommendation to the judge if the couple cannot reach an agreement. This power changes the mediator's role from one of neutral facilitator to one of evaluator or arbitrator.

Many states set stiff qualifications for these full-time mediators that include minimum levels of education, training, and experience. Accordingly, these mediators tend to be well educated, often with master's degrees in the social sciences and professional backgrounds in mental health or family counseling.

The following profile is of a mediator who works in court-connected programs and handles both regular civil disputes and custody and other family cases.

MEDIATOR PROFILE

Name: John Polanski

Title: Project Coordinator and Mediator

Mediation Service: Ashtabula County Joint Court Mediation Project, Jefferson, Ohio

Educational Background: Master's in education in community counseling, Youngstown State University, Ohio

Professional Affiliations: Practitioner-member and approved consultant, Association for Conflict Resolution

Number of Cases Handled in Career: 450–500

Current Caseload: Ten per week, including custody and visitation, juvenile truancy, contract disputes, and personal injury claims

Most Memorable Mediation Moment: "A divorcing couple in their twenties, whose main focus was, 'I'll get you, you so-and-so,' came in at 4:30 in the afternoon. I decided to challenge them and said, 'I'm willing to stay at the table as long as you are.' They took me up on it and didn't leave my office until 8:30 that night. During those four hours, I watched as they gradually chose to act in favor of their children rather than against each other."

Notable Features of My Conference Room: "Although it's a typical government room with fluorescent lights and white walls, we've made an effort to soften it with plenty of green plants and some art prints."

Favorite Expression Related to Conflict: "There's a better way to do this."

b. Small Claims Court Programs

Small claims courts are particularly good at handling cases in which the facts and the law are clear and each party's legal rights are plainly spelled out in writing, as in a lease or other contract. Many disputes between landlords and tenants involving nonpayment of rent or return of security deposits, for example, are routinely handled in small claims court. (All small claims courts have limitations on the size of cases they can hear. Upper limits range from about $2,000 to $7,500—with a few courts allowing cases with values as high as $10,000 to $15,000.)

Many of these cases might be well suited for mediation because they involve interpersonal conflicts and failures of communication. But small claims judges, like most other judges, don't have the time or the power (or, often, the inclination) to work with issues that aren't directly related to the legal question presented. As one judge explains, "Courts are not designed to solve angry feelings. It's like Joe Friday says: 'The facts ma'am, just the facts.'"

But these days, lots of small claims courts have mediation programs through which the litigants can try to settle their dispute before going in front of the judge. In most places, mediation is voluntary, but a few states and counties are now requiring parties to try mediation before they can go into the courtroom.

c. Prosecutor Mediation, Victim-Offender Reconciliation, and Restorative Justice Programs

In some courts, local public prosecutors or district attorneys' offices sponsor mediation programs. Unlike most court programs that focus on civil disputes, these programs mediate minor criminal complaints.

PROFILE: Prosecutor's Mediation in Cleveland

In Cleveland, the prosecutor's mediation program applies to "non-serious" crimes, such as theft of property valued at less than $300, telephone harassment, and personal menacing. Parties bringing these complaints are routinely encouraged to try mediation; mediations are conducted primarily by paid staff, with some volunteers participating as well. The program is voluntary and available at no charge. About 3,000 cases are mediated each year. Sessions last about 45 minutes to an hour. Agreements often call for parties to pay damages, return property, or avoid contacting each other. Nearly nine of ten cases result in a written settlement with no need for corrective follow-up within the next four weeks—a period the program's directors consider meaningful, given that many of the parties are in ongoing relationships.

Many cities and counties have "victim-offender reconciliation" or "restorative justice" programs. These programs may be affiliated with the prosecutor's office, or may be separate but receive most of their referrals from the prosecutors and police. Victim-offender reconciliation programs, also known as VORPs, are similar to the Cleveland prosecutor's program profiled above—they bring together the offender and victim in relatively minor crimes, with the assistance of a trained mediator, and give victims a chance to tell offenders how the crime affected them, ask questions of the offender, and be involved in creating a plan for moving forward, including restitution for any losses they suffered as a result of the crime.

Some restorative justice programs deal with major crimes, including violent crimes. These mediations are highly structured, and require the offender to take full responsibility for the crime before entering into the mediation process. Mediators are carefully trained in the special requirements of this complicated and very emotional process.

C. Government Mediation Programs

Many government departments and agencies use mediation programs to improve services and reduce administrative and litigation costs. At the federal level, for example, the Equal Employment Opportunity Commission (EEOC) uses mediators at regional offices to resolve workplace discrimination claims; the IRS employs mediators to help resolve claims between taxpayers and the agency; and the Farmer-Lender Mediation Program, run by the Farmers Home Administration, resolves cases between farmers and bankers. The National Association of Securities Dealers (NASD), an independent agency overseen by the U.S. Securities and Exchange Commission (SEC), makes mediators available to people who have disputes with their stock brokers. And Medicare has a new pilot program offering participants mediation for disputes with health care providers.

These programs are all independent of the Federal Mediation and Conciliation Service (FMCS)—a government agency that mediates contract disputes between employers and unions in the private and government sectors. (For more about the FMCS, the NASD, the EEOC, and other government mediation programs, see Chapter 6.)

Mediators with federal government programs tend to have backgrounds in law, labor relations, or human resources. Their jobs often command substantial salaries and require extensive training and experience. Even those who work on contract with government agencies as part-time mediators often have professional backgrounds and advanced degrees.

MEDIATOR PROFILE

Name: Mark Keppler

Title: Employment dispute mediator on contract with U.S. EEOC, San Francisco and Los Angeles regional offices

Regular Employment: Director of graduate programs and professor of human resource management at the Craig School of Business, California State University, Fresno

Educational Background: Law degree and master's degree in industrial relations, University of Wisconsin

Years Mediating: Four

Professional Affiliations: Member, Association for Conflict Resolution, American Bar Association

Number of Cases Mediated: 100

Current Caseload: Eight per month

Most Memorable Mediation Moment: "In a discrimination case, the employer and employee had reached a tentative agreement after caucusing. I left the employee for two minutes to get the employer's signature. When I returned, she informed me that she had talked to God while I was gone, and He said not to sign the agreement."

Notable Features of My Conference Room: "I generally use government offices. They range in quality from very good to very bad."

Favorite Expression Related to Conflict: "I'm not a judge. I'm a negotiations consultant. I'm here to help you reach your own agreement."

Government agencies that do not employ their own full-time mediators generally provide parties with lists of private mediators who have been screened for education, training, and subject-matter knowledge. For example, for its program mediating disputes between stock brokers and their clients, the NASD will refer parties only to outside mediators who have a substantial background in the securities industry as brokers, securities lawyers, or arbitrators.

At the state level, there are numerous mandatory and voluntary mediation programs as well. For example, every state must have a program for mediating special education disputes. Many states maintain special offices to monitor and coordinate mediation services throughout the state. Some actually provide services, often for public policy disputes that arise within the state and concern citizen groups and state agencies. But many just act as information clearinghouses. If you want to learn what mediation programs your state operates, the easiest way to find out is to contact the statewide mediation or dispute resolution office. A list of statewide offices appears in Appendix D.

D. Private Dispute Resolution Companies

Private dispute resolution is a growth industry. An increasing number of for-profit firms now compete to mediate cases such as contract disputes between businesses, construction cases, employment disputes involving wrongful discrimination and termination, and disputed insurance claims arising out of auto accidents and other mishaps. People and businesses involved in disputes like these—with complex legal and financial issues and substantial amounts of money involved—generally want to use a private firm with experienced, paid mediators rather than a community mediation center with volunteer mediators.

There are hundreds of private dispute resolution firms. Some operate at the national level, with offices in major cities; others are mid-size or small firms that operate regionally or locally.

The biggest national firm is JAMS (the name formerly stood for Judicial Arbitration & Mediation Services), which is headquartered in Irvine, California. Other national firms include Resolute Systems, Inc., headquartered in Milwaukee, Wisconsin; National Arbitration & Mediation, Inc., in Great Neck, New York; and National Mediation, in Sacramento, California. The American Arbitration Association, Inc., in New York City, and Arbitration Forums, Inc., in Tampa, Florida, are well-established nonprofit corporations that handle many of the same kinds of large, complex disputes as the for-profit companies. (Appendix C lists some of the larger national and regional private dispute resolution firms.)

1. How Private Dispute Resolution Companies Work

The primary functions of a private dispute resolution company are to

- provide a panel of trained and experienced mediators
- get all parties to agree to participate in mediation
- administer the mediation, including all paperwork, scheduling, and billing, and
- follow up with the parties after mediation if further dispute resolution services are needed.

Fees at most of the private firms generally start at a minimum of about $500 per party for a half-day mediation session. Costs can rise to thousands of dollars, depending on the complexity of the case and the length of time needed to resolve it—and on which mediator you choose.

Companies may have just one panel of mediators, or they may have several panels organized by the subject area of the mediators' specialty. For example, a company active in a number of different types of mediation may have a negligence panel composed of lawyers and judges familiar with accident claims; a health care panel composed of health care lawyers, physicians, and hospital administrators; and a construction panel composed of construction lawyers, engineers, architects, builders, and contractors of various specialties.

2. Mediators With Private Dispute Resolution Companies

Most of the larger private firms and many of the smaller ones maintain a list of people available to mediate disputes. Many panel members are former judges and practicing attorneys; others may have expertise in subjects such as engineering, health care, construction, and land use. Panel members usually work as independent contractors rather than employees of the company, although owners of smaller mediation firms often mediate cases. For example, two or three mediators may have gotten together to form a local dispute resolution company. They run the business, mediate some of the cases, and assign the rest to members of their panel of outside mediators. The bigger companies' panels sometimes include career mediators who have advanced mediation training and experience and who mediate full time, often with a specialty such as construction, business, or employment.

Some popular members of a company's panel may be selected to mediate weekly or a couple times a month; others may be selected just a few times a year. Mediators may be exclusive to one company, or they may appear on the panels of several companies. It all depends on how much they are in demand and whether any particular company is able to generate enough business to sign up mediators to work with that company exclusively. For example, all the retired judges on panels maintained by California-based JAMS work only for that firm. A person who wants one of these judges to mediate a case will have to go to JAMS. But a lawyer with mediation training in a mid-size city may appear on the panels of several local or regional companies, none of which provides enough business to warrant an exclusive relationship.

Private firms can differ hugely in terms of how much training and skill their mediators have. At one extreme, they often provide the most highly skilled career mediators. Yet paradoxically, it is also on these firms' panels where you are likely to find inexperienced mediators. This often results from the firms' habit of hiring big-name judges who have recently retired. Judges with little background or training in mediation may believe their role is just to "knock people's heads together" until they settle, as they did when they were on the bench. Similarly, a private firm's panel may include a lawyer-mediator who has specialized knowledge and a great reputation in a particular area of the law but who is untrained and inexperienced in mediation.

Following are two profiles—one of a retired judge who mediates with a private firm, and one of an executive and mediator at a private mediation firm called National Mediation in Sacramento.

MEDIATOR PROFILE

Name: Hon. Anton J. Valukas

Title: Mediator-arbitrator on contract with Resolute Systems, Inc., Chicago

Regular Employment: Retired supervising judge, Pretrial Mediation Division, Circuit Court of Cook County, Chicago

Educational Background: Law degree, DePaul College of Law; L.L.B., J.D., Chicago

Years Mediating with Private Firm: Six

Number of Cases Handled: 300–400

Current Caseload: Four to five per month, including malpractice, personal injury, contracts, and general civil matters

Most Memorable Mediation Moment: "A ten-year-old boy was hit by a truck and left a paraplegic. Four years later, the parties came to mediation. They later told me they had never intended to settle. But after six hours they reached an agreement. The boy was present. Though he had difficulty holding up his head, when we settled he grasped my hand, gave me a smile, and said 'Thanks.'"

Favorite Expression Related to Conflict: "In all my cases, I sit the parties down, get acquainted, and say, 'There are three things I can assure you of: (1) I am neutral and this playing field is as level as this table; (2) I will never violate a confidence or a trust; and (3) I'll never tell you my age.' That relaxes them."

MEDIATOR PROFILE

Name: James MacPherson

Title: Vice President and Mediator, National Mediation, Inc., Sacramento, California

Former Employment: Mediator and Mediation Administrator

Educational Background: B.A., advanced degree, Ombudsman training; mediation training

Years Practicing as Mediator: Ten

Number of Cases Handled in Career: Several hundred; in addition, trains thousands of lawyers, adjusters, HR reps and other professionals in conflict resolution; has conceived and directed numerous ADR programs

Current Caseload: Varies from week to week; cases include civil, commercial, business, contract, construction, workplace, real estate, civil rights, personal injury

Notable Features of My Conference Room: Plenty of natural light from windows and very comfortable chairs; flipchart and dry erase board.

Philosophy of Mediation: Deliver an efficient, effective early resolution on a cost-effective basis—premediation work is essential and, along with effective case management, dramatically increases the likelihood of reaching a resolution.

Personal Values in Mediation: "The parties always have the answers."

Favorite Quotes About Conflict: "Not everything that's faced can be changed, but nothing can be changed until it is faced." (James Baldwin.) "No doubt there are other important things in life besides conflict, but there are not many other things so inevitably interesting." (Robert Lynd.)

E. Independent Mediators in Private Practice

Independent mediators in private practice work on their own, although some also participate in nonexclusive panels with private dispute resolution firms and/or court-connected panels. But they are not employees of these companies or services. Independent mediators set their own fees, handle their own paperwork, keep their own schedules, and often develop and use their own mediation rules.

It can be economical for disputants to use an independent mediator when they don't need or want to pay for the help of a private dispute resolution company—for example, when all the parties agree to mediate and are able to arrange the session themselves by calling the mediator directly.

Fees range from $100 to $300 an hour for independent mediators who work at the local level and have a general practice, to $1,500 to $5,000 (or even more) a day for full-time mediators who operate nationally and specialize in large, complex disputes in areas such as business and construction.

In this section we'll separate independent mediators into two very broad categories—specialty and general mediators.

1. Specialty Mediators

Some mediators make a good living specializing in specific areas—from family matters to large, complex cases, such as those involving business ownership and employee relations, construction, patents and copyrights, environmental issues, or land use.

a. Divorce and Family Mediators

Many full-time independent mediators handle divorce and family mediation as their sole area of practice. Divorce mediation is probably the most well-established specialty in the field of mediation—in many large and medium-size cities, more than 25% of divorcing couples go through mediation, so there is a steady demand for these services. The skills that mediators develop in working with divorcing couples also translate well to other interpersonal disputes, such as those involving family members, friends, and coworkers, and many divorce mediators like to round out their practice with such cases.

Most divorce mediators practice by themselves or sometimes as part of a small group. Divorce mediation lends itself to independent practice because a sole practitioner can build a practice by contacting the major sources of case referrals in the community, such as therapists, clergy, and divorce lawyers. And the mediator can charge enough ($125–$150 per hour is typical in a mid-size city, but some very experienced mediators charge much more) to make a living.

Unlike court-connected divorce mediation, in which program administrators assign a mediator to work with a couple, in private mediation couples voluntarily retain the services of a mediator they choose themselves. The couple can decide to make their mediation comprehensive and cover all the issues in their breakup, including parenting and financial issues, or limit it to certain issues, usually custody and visitation. Anywhere from two to a half-dozen or more sessions may be required, depending on the number and complexity of issues addressed, and the dynamics between the parties.

In theory, anyone can hang out a shingle and claim to be a divorce mediator. Many divorce mediators also practice divorce law, or used to, and have a good working knowledge of the field. But any divorce mediator who is serious about building a practice will get some training—often a standard 40-hour training course with a trainer approved by the Association for Conflict Resolution (ACR), a national organization that includes what formerly had been the Academy of Family Mediators. (For more information on training, see Chapter 4.)

PROFILE: Family Mediators

Some time ago, the former Academy of Family Mediators (before it merged into ACR) did a survey of its membership and found that, of nearly 2,000 active members,

- 40% have a background in law, 30% in therapy or social work.
- 80% hold a master's degree, a Ph.D., or law degree.
- 70% are between the ages of 40 and 59.
- 60% are female.
- 70% are in solo practice.

Here's a profile of a fairly typical family mediator and her practice.

MEDIATOR PROFILE

Name: Dolly Hinckley

Title: Divorce and family mediator

Mediation Service: Self-employed, doing business as Divorce Mediation Associates in Rochester, New York

Educational Background: B.S. in business administration (management), University of Buffalo, Buffalo, New York

Professional Affiliations: Advanced practitioner-member and approved consultant, ACR; Board of Directors, New York State Council on Divorce Mediation

Number of Cases Handled in Career: 1,000+

Current Caseload: 12

Most Memorable Mediation Moment: "A bright, middle-aged couple with two children, ages three and ten, bickered intensively during five months of divorce mediation. At the last session, after concluding an agreement and committing to work cooperatively in the future to parent their children, in my presence—spontaneously and triumphantly—they hugged each other."

Notable Features of My Conference Room: "I use a large, comfortable room in my home decorated with items from my travels around the world, including two 30-inch-tall African fertility statues."

Favorite Expression Related to Conflict: "Conflict is inevitable, but fighting is a choice."

b. Other Specialty Mediators

There are other fields besides divorce where mediators may specialize. A prime example is construction cases, which frequently turn on issues involving specialized knowledge of engineering or architecture. Often, the parties in those cases want a mediator with particular expertise in the field. Some specialty mediators are in great demand and travel extensively, hearing cases around the country.

Developing a specialty can be a great marketing strategy. If you have an area in which you are already an expert, redirecting your skills toward mediation might be the way to go. But being a successful mediator in a limited field requires good mediation skills and strong entrepreneurial drive.

We'll talk more about what it takes to develop a full-time practice as a specialty mediator in Chapter 5. In the meantime, here's a profile of a mediator who has found a niche in the construction field.

MEDIATOR PROFILE

Name: Joseph Grynbaum

Title: Construction mediator

Mediation Service: Self-employed, doing business as "Mediation Resolution International," based in West Hartford, Connecticut; publishes email newsletter on developments in the construction industry.

Educational Background: B.S. in mechanical engineering, Caulfield Institute of Technology, Melbourne, Australia

Years in Practice as Mediator: Three

Professional Affiliations: Member, ACR; associate member, Section on Dispute Resolution, American Bar Association

Number of Cases Handled in Career: Six

Current Caseload: Two

Most Memorable Mediation Moment: "After a successful mediation, the lawyer for one side said, 'Going into this mediation after three years of belligerent litigation, I could never imagine we'd settle.'"

Notable Feature of My Mediation Sessions: "I have a 'no buts' rule. I ban the word 'but' because it dilutes the positive aspect of a statement made to the opposite side. The rule also gives everyone a shared role in controlling each other's slippages during the session."

Favorite Expression Related to Conflict: "An ounce of mediation is worth a pound of arbitration and a ton of litigation."

2. General Mediators

Some mediators earn their living with a general mediation practice, taking a variety of business and legal disputes—essentially, whatever comes through the door. Until recently, this kind of practice was rare because there just was not enough business to keep a general mediator busy. Fortunately, as mediation has continued to grow in popularity, a modest but increasing number of mediators are now able to make a living with a general practice. (For more on establishing and running a general mediation practice, see Chapter 5.)

A Note on Part-Time Mediation

Some independent mediators work only part time, while relying on some other profession or occupation such as law, business, or social work, for their primary income. Part-time mediators may be in private practice, or they may work through the panels of private dispute resolution companies, court-connected or government agency programs, or programs run by professional associations to which they belong.

Some part-time mediators are well trained and highly skilled, and there's nothing wrong with being actively engaged in another line of work and mediating on the side. But some part-time mediators don't take mediation seriously, have received little or no training, and view part-time mediation either as an easy way to pick up extra cash or to add some class to their resume. If you are trying to start a mediation practice by adding mediation to your current work, make sure that you take the time to get quality training and enough experience so that when you do have the opportunity to sit at the head of the table as a mediator—even if it's just on occasion—the people seated to your right and your left receive competent, professional services.

F. Corporate, Association, and In-House Mediation Programs

Many organizations, large and small, are starting to establish mediation programs for their employees or members. These programs and services don't generally employ large numbers of mediators, but they can offer interesting challenges to mediators who happen to have a connection with the sponsoring organization.

As professional associations and other membership groups seek new ways to serve their members, many have established mediation programs. For example, the National Association of Realtors began the Home Buyer/Home Seller Dispute Resolution Program to help mediate claims by home buyers and sellers against real estate agents. Similarly, the National Association of Electrical Engineers started a program to help resolve claims against its members. These and similar programs often train current or retired members of the associations to act as mediators. To see if an association to which you have a connection has a mediation program, check the group's website or contact the national office. Many such groups are headquartered in Washington, DC, New York City, or other large cities.

Many large businesses, looking for ways to improve productivity and worker satisfaction, have discovered the value of in-house dispute resolution programs to improve communication among staff, resolve conflicts, and reduce the likelihood of violence in the workplace. Typically, selected staff members (managers and employees of different ages, ethnic backgrounds, and job descriptions) are trained to act as mediators. When disputes arise between or among employees, the disputants are invited (or sometimes required) to go to mediation conducted by one of the staff mediators.

PROFILE: Bally's Las Vegas Takes a Gamble on Mediation Program

Bally's, a Las Vegas resort with 4,000 employees, established an in-house mediation program. Twenty-four staff members, representing a cross section of employees from senior management to support staff (and including union members), went through training with the local community mediation center. The training included techniques for handling employee disputes, interdepartmental conflicts, and supervisor-employee disputes. A company spokeswoman said the program reduced management time spent dealing with internal company conflicts.

Do you think you want to mediate within your company? To find out if the corporation you work for has an in-house mediation program, inquire with the human resources office or in-house counsel.

G. Specialized Mediation Programs

As mediation gains in popularity, some specialized groups, including business trade organizations and religious groups, have begun to develop their own networks of mediation services. The following are just a few examples of specialized programs.

Asian Pacific American Dispute Resolution Center. This organization provides mediation and conciliation services in Asian Pacific languages, including Chinese, Korean, Japanese, Vietnamese, and Tagalog. The center handles ethnic disputes, as well as domestic, housing, neighborhood, employment, and business conflicts, and matters involving race relations. Disputants are asked to pay nominal processing and hourly fees, but fees are waived for those unable to pay. The center primarily serves Los Angeles County but assists those outside the area by conducting telephone mediation and by making referrals nationally to mediators or translators fluent in Asian Pacific languages. For information, contact the Center at 1145 Wilshire Blvd., Suite 100, Los Angeles, CA 90017; 213-250-8190, or visit their website at www.apadrc.org.

Peacemaker Ministries. This national group, with a network of trained conciliators around the country, uses Christian biblical principles of conflict resolution to mediate disputes. The organization trains and certifies its own conciliators; the group includes people from many professional and work backgrounds: lawyers, mental health counselors, clergy, homemakers, and business people. For information, contact Peacemaker Ministries, 1537 Avenue D, Suite 352, Billings, MT 59102; 406-256-1583, or visit their website: www.HISPEACE.org.

Lesbian and Gay Community Services Center: Center Mediation Services/Project Resolve. This program helps lesbian, gay, bisexual, transgender, and people with HIV-AIDS and their families to resolve conflicts outside the court system. Matters commonly addressed include relationship breakups, child custody and visitation issues, and disputes within and among community groups. Mediators include lawyers, mental health professionals, teachers, activists, and health care workers. All services are free of charge. The group operates in the New York City area and can provide referrals to similar services nationally. For more information, contact Center Mediation Services/ Project Resolve at 208 West 13th St., New York, NY 10011; 212-620-7310, or visit their website: www.gaycenter.org.

Arts Resolution Services: This is a national collaborative project funded by the NEA, several foundations, and government agencies, to coordinate dispute resolution procedures for arts organizations and individual artists throughout the country. Check your local arts agencies for information about dispute resolution programs for the arts in your area.

Mediator Training and Education

To those who have never done it, mediation can look deceptively easy: you just sit at the head of the table and talk sense to people until they agree to be reasonable. It can look so easy, in fact, that some people think they can jump right in to mediating without being trained. In our view, this is a mistake. If you want to mediate, you need to be trained. It's that simple.

Fortunately, mediator training is usually a stimulating, enjoyable experience. In fact, many people who don't intend to mediate professionally take the training anyway just to learn the skills, which they can then use in their jobs or their personal lives.

As mediation has grown in popularity, mediator training has become a good-size industry. Training is now offered through community mediation centers, private dispute resolution companies, and colleges and universities. A growing number of independent trainers travel around the country giving seminars.

Which training you take, where you take it, and with whom are important considerations. In this chapter, we'll examine basic mediator training, divorce mediation and other specialized training, and degree programs in dispute resolution. We'll start by looking at licensing and certification issues.

A. Licensing and Certification

There is a lot of confusion about what *certification* and *licensing* mean as applied to mediators. There's also a lot of rapid change and a great deal of debate on these issues in the field of mediation. But before we get to that, let's define our terms.

The term "licensing" in general refers to official authorization, in the form of a license from a governmental or administrative agency (the state bar, the state real estate commissioner, the board of cosmetology), that allows you to do something—practice law, buy or sell real estate, or open a hair salon. Currently, there is no licensing requirement for mediators in any state.

Some people think licensing mediators is a good idea because it would help protect consumers against unqualified practitioners. Others oppose licensing because they say it would exclude some of the most talented people, who may lack some required educational background but have natural skills as mediators. The debate goes on. It seems pretty likely that in the future at least some states will enact licensing requirements for mediators.

Certification is a bit more complicated. For example, both authors of this book are certified mediators, but what does that mean? It means only that they took a training program (or more than one) and that the trainer issued a certificate attesting to successful completion of the program. In many circumstances, a certificate is required to mediate in a particular setting. For example, most mediation centers and many court-connected programs require that you have a certificate from a specified training program before you can mediate there. Similarly, some online dispute resolution services—SquareTrade, for example, which handles many disputes generated by online auctions—now certify their mediators and use only certified contractors. If you want to get referrals through these types of programs and services, you'll need to get certified. But if all you want is to conduct a private mediation practice, you may not want to do any more than just getting certified through whatever training you take to learn to mediate.

In an effort to make certification more meaningful, the Association for Conflict Resolution (ACR) is part of a movement to establish national standards for certification—which would be voluntary, unlike a license. Proposed requirements include a specified number of hours of training and experience, along with completion of a written "knowledge assessment."

B. Where to Get Basic Training

A word of caution: many people get enthusiastic about mediation and want to jump right into opening a practice in a specialty area—often divorce mediation, because it's well known. Our advice is to take it a bit slower—first, find out whether you like mediating and are any good at it. Begin with some basic training and find ways to practice before you learn a specialty and hang out a shingle on your own.

By basic training, we mean an introductory course that covers the essentials of mediation: the psychology of human conflict, negotiation theory, techniques of listening and speaking, laws of mediation and confidentiality, mediator ethics, and the practical skills needed to conduct a mediation session. Most trainings use a combination of lectures, videos, demonstrations, and role-playing exercises—the last being possibly the most important component and one you should definitely not forgo.

You have two main options for getting trained as a mediator: sign up with a community mediation center and get trained through the center's program, or take a training course through a private mediation training provider. We'll look at each of these in turn.

1. Training at a Community Center

One of the best deals available is a basic mediator training course at a nonprofit community mediation center. As we explained in Chapter 3, community mediation centers are tax-supported agencies that provide free or low-cost mediation services to the general public. There are hundreds of centers nationwide; check the yellow pages under "mediation" and you'll probably find one where you live or close by.

The primary advantages of training at a community mediation center are (1) cost, and (2) the opportunity to apprentice and stay involved with the center to gain experience and contribute to your community. Community mediation centers usually don't charge as much as private training providers, and some even provide free training in exchange for a promise that you will mediate a certain number of cases there as a volunteer after you are trained. (Some centers charge a fee for their training but then rebate it after you fulfill the volunteer commitment.)

Beyond cost savings, the best reason to get trained at a community mediation center is that many centers offer a post-training apprenticeship or other opportunities for you to practice your new skills on real cases. "Once you get out of that training, you're not ready to mediate," advises Craig Coletta, coordinator for the National Association for Community Mediation. "You've learned the skills, but you have no fluency in them. Apprenticeship gives trainees the opportunity to apply mediation skills in real situations in a way they can't learn just in role-plays."

Make sure apprenticeships are available. In most places, you can probably call a community mediation center today and be scheduled for training within the next couple of months. However, some centers accept lots of people for training, even when their caseloads might not allow those new volunteers to mediate right away. So before you sign up for training, confirm with the center that you'll be able to participate in the apprenticeship program and get started mediating fairly soon.

At community mediation centers, training is usually conducted by staff members, often assisted by some of the center's own experienced mediators. Some training is excellent; some is just adequate. It's fair to say that at some centers, particularly the smaller ones, the quality of individual trainers may not be as consistently high as you would find with full-time, professional trainers at for-profit firms.

Still, the other advantages of training at a community mediation center— low cost, accessibility, and opportunity for apprenticeship—may outweigh concerns about the quality of individual trainers. In fact, the use of multiple trainers at most centers offers its own advantage: you get to hear about mediation from a variety of points of view. And, if you complete the training and apprenticeship and find you like mediation, you can—and probably should—take a more advanced training with an outstanding national or regional trainer.

2. Training With Private Training Providers

There are lots of private, for-profit training companies that will teach you the basics of mediation. Their fees will be substantial—anywhere from $750 to $1,500 or more. The curriculum will often be very similar to that at a community mediation center's training—you will learn the psychology of conflict, communication skills, mediation theory, and role-playing practice.

Given that, why would you pay more for these trainings? The main reason is that in many cases, you will have more information about the trainers—their background, skills, and mediation experience—in a private training course. At a community mediation center, the trainers may be volunteers or center staff, and some of them may be teaching because they are good at teaching, or because they are available, rather than because they have extensive experience or excellent mediation skills. With commercial mediation training, you will probably be able to see complete resumes for the trainer(s), learn about their background and experience, and see what other trainees say about the programs.

The other advantage to a private mediation training program is that the time and location may be more convenient for you. If you live somewhere without a nearby community mediation center, or if the center near you has enough volunteers and isn't planning a training during the time frame that will work for you, a private program may meet your needs better.

Appendix D contains a list of statewide mediation offices. You can try contacting the office in your state for more information on training—both through private trainers and at community mediation centers.

C. What to Expect in Basic Training

Whether you choose to go through basic training with a community mediation center or a private, commercial training program, the mediation training itself will pretty much be the same. Usually, you'll have between 25 and 40 hours of class time. The number of hours will depend on local rules and whether state law sets a minimum. For a long time, 25 hours was typical, but today, as more topics like cross-cultural differences and mediator ethics are added to the curriculum, 40 hours is emerging as the standard. Training may be held on consecutive weekdays or over two or three weekends.

Mediators Are Interesting Folks

One nice aspect of training, especially at a community mediation center, is the diverse mix of people you're likely to find there. At one recent session that Peter attended, there were 13 trainees, ranging in age from about 20 to 70. Among them were two college students, a retired social worker, a mechanical engineer, the director of a service program for mentally disabled adults, the human resources director of a large business corporation, a financial planner, a librarian, a paralegal, a community activist, and an accountant.

Only a few of those attending expected to become professional mediators; most just wanted to volunteer as mediators or hoped to get new skills that would be useful to them in their jobs. For example, the financial planner wanted mediation skills to use in helping clients deal with family conflicts over financial goals; the paralegal believed she could mediate minor harassment cases that come in to the law office where she worked; the community activist hoped negotiating skills would help her deal more effectively with local government officials. One trainee had just completed basic mediator training with a private firm but realized he had no opportunity to test out his new skills. He was taking basic training all over again at the community mediation center so that he could participate in the apprenticeship program.

I. Content of the Training

Your training course is likely to begin with a set of exercises designed to get you thinking about conflict and communication. Here are a few examples from mediation trainings that the authors have attended:

- **A common opening exercise** asks trainees to view a simple line drawing that depicts, depending on how you look at it, either a young girl or an old woman. In one recent training, half the group saw the young girl and several saw the old woman, but a few others saw what they insisted was a rabbit; one person claimed to see a convertible with its hood up, driving off a cliff. The trainer effectively used the exercise to illustrate how reasonable people can look at the same thing but see it differently, just as the parties in mediation will insist on their own versions of the truth in their dispute. "Perception is a person's reality," stressed the trainer. "It is their truth." The group then generated a list of factors that can affect people's perceptions: age, gender, ethnicity, religion, culture, education, and socioeconomic status, to name just a few.
- **A related exercise** is designed to help participants learn about their own prejudices. The trainer describes a fictitious person: her looks, clothes, occupation, and manner of speech. Trainees are then asked to answer a series of questions about the personal habits, family life, political beliefs, and financial situation of the person described. When trainees compare their answers, they find that what they have described are simply their own assumptions and prejudices about people. The exercise helps teach mediators to be aware of their own prejudices, particularly during the opening stages of mediation when one may be tempted to form opinions of the disputants based on appearance or superficial information.
- **A communication exercise** that helps trainees see firsthand how effective it is to ask open, curious questions, begins with the participants pairing off and choosing one of a list of topics prepared by the trainers. Each pair is then instructed to argue strenuously, with each person taking a side and sticking to it, refusing to listen to the other person's point of view and engaging in typically polarizing acts like putting hands on hips, rolling eyes, or even turning away. After everyone's had a great time exercising all their defensive communication methods, they are asked to try again, this time asking each other curious questions about the other point of view. While it might seem obvious that the latter method is the more effective way to

communicate, experiencing the contrast in the midst of the learning process can be most useful.

- **In communities with ethnically diverse populations,** significant training time may be spent on how cultural differences can affect conflict and communication. In some cultures, for example, making direct eye contact is considered disrespectful, but in others, avoiding direct eye contact is considered suspect. Put people from both cultures at the same mediation table, and one may think the other is being disrespectful while the other thinks the first is lying. Similarly, lots of people assume that a mediator, in order to be neutral and credible, should be unknown to both parties. But others, because of their own cultural background, might consider that ridiculous. How can you help solve our problem, they might ask, if you don't know either of us?

Usually, the first and greatest focus in training exercises is communication skills (specifically, listening carefully and speaking skillfully). To sharpen listening skills—and get to know each other—trainees, working in pairs, might be asked to tell each other their life stories in two minutes of nonstop talking. The listeners are asked to pay careful attention, make it clear that they are listening attentively, and then repeat back as much of the story as they can recall.

Basic training often includes a discussion of the various methods of dispute resolution, including negotiation, fact finding, conciliation, mediation, arbitration, and litigation. Some of the legal issues that arise in mediation are discussed: rules of confidentiality and how they apply to mediators, what a mediator should do if information received during the hearing suggests child or spouse abuse, and how to help parties write a settlement agreement that will be legally binding.

What You Won't Learn in Mediation Training

It's interesting to notice what's not included in basic training: the legal rules of family law, consumer law, or property rights. Even though these issues are likely to arise, especially at community mediation centers, it's not the mediator's role to act as lawyer or judge, and mediator training isn't law school. When these matters do come up in an actual case, mediators mostly have to rely on their own general knowledge or be able to pick up the basics from the parties themselves or in consultation with the center's staff. (Training for divorce mediation, which we discuss later, does include instruction in family law, tax law, and other relevant areas. And if you're going to specialize in a particular field, you'll need to have the required knowledge.)

In a typical 25- or 40-hour basic training course, fully half the time will likely be spent learning and practicing the actual skills you will need to conduct a two-party mediation. Lectures will be supported by videos of actual or simulated cases and role playing exercises in which you will get to try out your skills on mock cases. In these exercises, trainees will break up into groups of three or four, with one practicing the role of the mediator while the others take on the role of parties (or, if there's an extra person, possibly a witness).

Role-plays will be designed to improve listening and negotiating skills, to reveal personal prejudices, or to develop an ability to detect hidden interpersonal conflicts among the parties.

In a typical role-play, for example, the trainee playing the mediator is told that the case involves a property-line dispute between two neighbors—a man and a woman. What the trainee is not told, however, is that the two neighbors many years ago were close friends but then had a falling out when the wife of one quarreled with the husband of the other over child-rearing issues. The dispute about the property line, although real, is just the latest expression of continuing distrust between the neighbors because of the earlier break in their friendship.

In the mock mediation, the trainees playing the feuding neighbors know the history, but the trainee playing the mediator does not and must discover it through careful listening and questioning. The goal is not to make the neighbors friends again but to help them come to terms with the break in their relationship so they not only can resolve this property-line dispute but also can agree to live peacefully as neighbors. This type of role-play helps sharpen important skills a mediator will need to resolve real cases.

Basic training may conclude with a session on how to help the parties draft an effective settlement agreement, a discussion of mediator ethics, and the record-keeping requirements of the particular mediation center where the trainees will apprentice as volunteer mediators.

2. Post-Training Apprenticeship

This section applies to community mediation training—most private training programs don't offer the opportunity for apprenticeship or practice, although some mediation trainers will work with trainees as consultants. (See "How to Get Help With Your Practice," below.)

Some community mediation centers have formal apprenticeship programs; in others, the post-training practice is somewhat less formal. At most community mediation centers, however, your introduction to actual mediations will begin with observing experienced mediators as they hear actual cases. Typically, centers require silent observation of three or more mediations. The trainee attends with the permission of the disputants and is bound by the same rules of confidentiality as the mediator. This experience exposes the trainee to different styles of mediation and to some of the issues that come up in real cases.

The next step is co-mediation. During an actual mediation, the trainee sits next to the experienced mediator and practices conducting various parts of the session. The trainee may, for example, deliver the opening statement—the first stage of mediation, in which the mediator explains the structure and rules of the mediation. (For more on the stages of mediation, see Chapter 1.)

The final step of the apprenticeship comes when trainees are allowed to mediate cases on their own. An experienced mediator observes the session and steps in if the trainee needs help. The observer takes notes on the trainee's technique to review with him or her afterwards. Several solo mediations may be scheduled until both the trainee and the staff of the mediation center feel confident that the trainee can handle cases alone.

When the apprenticeship is completed, the trainee is ready to mediate. (If watching a few cases and then handling a few under supervision doesn't sound like a lot of preparation, consider that lawyers can go into court alone on their first day after being admitted to the bar without ever setting foot in a courtroom or handling a case under the supervision of an experienced attorney.)

The apprenticeship period won't be exactly the same everywhere. Some community mediation centers use panels of two or three mediators for every mediation. In that case, a new mediator, after observing a case or two, would be placed on a panel with more experienced mediators and allowed to learn by doing.

How to Get Help With Your Practice

If you are trained by a private mediation trainer, you won't have the apprenticeship opportunities that are offered by community mediation centers. But you might have other ways to get support and advice as you begin mediating. Sometimes, the person who trains you will consult with you (usually for a fee) on cases that you mediate on your own. If you sign up with a court-connected program such as a small claims court program, there might be an administrator who can give you some help—or, you might be able to mediate your first few cases together with someone more experienced who will be willing to give you feedback. Finally, if you know experienced mediators, ask them if they'll help you out by working with you or consulting with you on cases.

D. Divorce Mediation

As we've noted, many mediators specialize in divorce. The demand is already strong and continues to grow in that area, and training programs dedicated to divorce mediation are readily available.

In theory, anyone can hang out a shingle and claim to be a divorce mediator, but if trying to mediate general cases without training is a mistake, trying to be a divorce mediator without training is a much, much bigger one. Mediating divorces requires an understanding of family law, tax law, pension rules, and the psychology of families in crisis—to name just a few complex subjects. Divorce mediators deal with couples at one of the most difficult and emotionally charged times of their lives. Divorce mediation is nothing to play around with, and an untrained mediator can cause great harm.

1. Association for Conflict Resolution Divorce Mediation Training

If you want to become a divorce mediator, you absolutely must get the skills and knowledge to do it well. Probably the best way to prepare yourself is by taking a training course approved by the Association for Conflict Resolution (ACR). ACR is a national, nonprofit organization that sets standards for the training and practice of divorce and family mediation. Training programs approved by ACR must meet detailed requirements for course content and presentation.

An ACR-approved training course for divorce mediation must do all of the following:

- include 40 hours of instruction spread over a minimum of five days
- include at least six hours of role-playing exercises
- provide trainees with a comprehensive manual of written materials and forms
- teach general mediation skills with demonstrations and role-playing exercises focused on family issues
- instruct how to screen for situations in which mediation might not be appropriate for the parties, including when domestic violence is present, and
- address the consequences of separation and divorce on adults and children, and cover issues of parenting, division of marital assets and liabilities, spousal maintenance and child support, insurance, pensions, and tax filing.

You can expect to pay between $800 and $1,500 for ACR-approved training. Some trainers offer a slight discount if you sign up early and pay the full fee in advance. In addition to 40-hour divorce mediation training, the ACR also approves 30-hour training courses in family mediation that cover parenting, custody, and other family matters, but omit the financial issues covered in divorce mediation training. Fees for family mediation training are likely to be lower than those for divorce mediation training.

Divorce Mediation Isn't for Everyone

One co-author of this book is a family mediator. For her, the experience of working with couples going through a breakup is enormously satisfying. "People are in such a difficult place, and yet they work so hard to get past that and to find a resolution that works for the whole family. It's really an honor to help people work with the sometimes complicated legal rules and to support them as they try to bring their best selves to the mediation process. It's a really challenging area, but worth it."

The other has this to say about his experience with divorce mediation training: "Some years ago, I took a full 40-hour, ACR-approved training course with the intention of doing divorce mediation. But even before the training was completed, I knew I would not mediate divorces. I just found it too painful to deal with some of the issues, particularly those involving children. I have high regard for mediators who help divorcing couples through such a difficult time, but I could not do it. I also saw that being a competent divorce mediator would require me to keep up with pension and tax laws, and local court decisions involving spousal maintenance, child support, and custody. With my other obligations, I knew I could not devote the necessary time and attention to those topics."

Remember when we said that mediation can be stressful and emotionally draining? Well, divorce mediation can be all that and more. The payoff is the satisfaction of helping people through a really challenging time in their lives—but if you don't have a lot of patience and a well-developed ability to separate yourself from your work at the end of the day, think twice before choosing divorce as your mediation specialty.

If you're considering becoming a divorce mediator, check out the ACR website at www.acrnet.org. ACR has some excellent materials that will demonstrate in detail what divorce mediation looks like, including a 20-minute videotape, "Mediation: It's Up to You." The tape simulates a mediation between a couple who have one small child and own a business together. (The session is simulated, but the mediator is a real, nationally recognized divorce mediator.) The tape is available for $59.95—a bargain if it helps you decide whether or not to take training that lasts five days and costs upwards of $1,000.

Perhaps not surprisingly, many people get interested in becoming divorce mediators after having had their own divorces mediated. It's as good an introduction to the field as any, but some mediation trainers caution that you should wait a while before going ahead with training. They want you to be sure your attraction to the field is a genuine career move and not just an emotional reaction to your own divorce.

2. Choosing a Divorce Mediation Trainer

When ACR approves a training course, technically it approves only the course content; it does not endorse the individual trainer. Nevertheless, even to submit a course for ACR approval, a trainer must meet the criteria for practitioner-level status in ACR. This means the trainer has taken at least 60 hours of ACR-approved training, had a minimum of 100 hours of face-to-face mediation experience, had sample case reports reviewed by other mediators, and completed 20 hours of continuing education every two years.

Currently, ACR maintains a list of about 50 trainers around the country who offer approved courses. The list shows trainers based in about 20 states and several Canadian provinces. Some offer training on a regular schedule outside their home states, and some will conduct a training anywhere if a person interested in being trained can recruit a minimum number of participants (usually four to six).

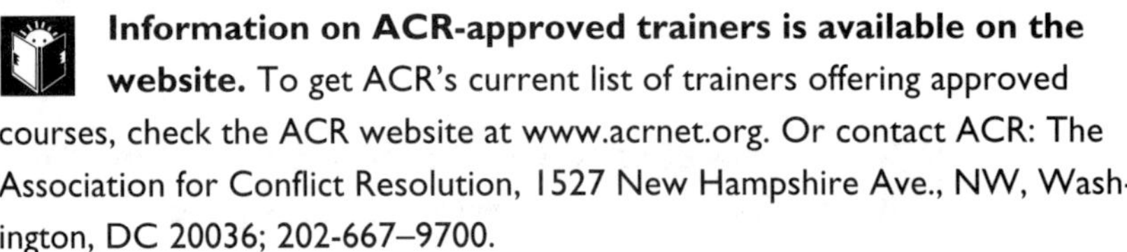

Information on ACR-approved trainers is available on the website. To get ACR's current list of trainers offering approved courses, check the ACR website at www.acrnet.org. Or contact ACR: The Association for Conflict Resolution, 1527 New Hampshire Ave., NW, Washington, DC 20036; 202-667–9700.

Once you get ACR's list of trainers, take some time to consider which trainer to use. Obviously, location and cost will be factors, but choosing a trainer should involve more than just considerations of cost and location. Your trainer will shape your early practice and may become an important long-term mentor.

Some Tips for Choosing a Divorce Mediation Trainer

- If possible, try to meet the prospective trainer—or at least talk on the phone—before signing up. Does the personal chemistry feel right? Does the trainer seem enthusiastic or somewhat stale after mediating and training for decades?
- Get a sense of the trainer's focus. Does the trainer emphasize the economics of divorce or the parenting and emotional aspects? How does the trainer's approach compare with what you anticipate will be your own? You and the trainer don't have to have the same approach—complementary interests can be good—but it's useful to know going in whether you differ or not.
- Ask for references to others who have completed training with this trainer and are now practicing. If the trainer lives in your town, ask how the trainer works with trainees who set up practice locally. Soon you will be direct competitors for the same clientele. Is the trainer supportive of this? Will the trainer consult with or supervise you as you begin practicing?
- Ask whether the trainer's manual will include forms for you to use in setting up and marketing your own practice. (You can purchase these elsewhere, but it saves a lot of time and money if the trainer provides them in the manual, and this is another clue as to how supportive of your practice the trainer may be.)

E. Other Specialized Training

In addition to divorce and family mediation, there are opportunities for specialized mediation training in other areas in which you may have a particular interest. Remember, training in specialized fields should come only after you complete basic mediator training and get some experience.

We list below some of the more popular areas of specialization. Specialty training is offered by private training firms, conflict resolution groups, or professional associations.

1. Health Care

The growing number of disputes arising out of the delivery of health care services has created a demand for conflict resolution in this field. Claims against doctors, hospitals, and health maintenance organizations, disputes between doctors and insurers, and grievances between health care workers and their employers all might end up at the mediation table.

Several programs are available to train people to mediate health care disputes. One, offered by the American Health Lawyers Association, is open to both lawyers and nonlawyers, including physicians, nurses, and health care executives. For information, contact the American Health Lawyers Association at 202-833-1100 or visit their website at www.healthlawyers.org.

The Harvard School of Public Health offers courses to help health care professionals improve negotiation and conflict resolution skills in areas such as bioethical conflicts, interhospital disputes, interprofessional disputes, and community health matters. For information on current course offerings, check the website of the Public Health Practice section of the university's website at www.hsph.harvard.edu/php, or call 617-496–0865.

The federal Medicare program has a new mediation program through which Medicare beneficiaries can mediate concerns about quality of care with their doctors or other health care providers. As the program grows, more mediators will be trained to conduct these sessions. You can find information about the program by calling 800-841-1602 or checking the Web at www.lumetra.com.

2. Environment and Public Policy

Issues including land use, zoning, environmental protection, and the siting of highways and public buildings come under the general heading of "public policy" disputes. Many colleges that offer advanced degrees in conflict resolution (see Section F, below) also offer courses on mediating environmental and public policy disputes.

CDR Associates of Boulder, Colorado, offers several courses regularly on these topics. Contact CDR at 1–800-Mediate or on the Web at www.mediate.org. And the U.S. Institute for Environmental Conflict Resolution in Tucson is a government-sponsored organization that offers training in this field. Call 520-670-5299 or check the website at www.ecr.gov.

3. Employment

Workplace disputes involving termination, discrimination, and other labor issues own an increasing share of the national mediation caseload. The U.S. Equal Employment Opportunity Commission (EEOC) trains mediators to hear discrimination cases brought by those who file charges with the Commission. Contact the agency's national headquarters in Washington, DC, at 202-663-4900 or through their website at www.eeoc.gov.

Private training firms such as CDR Associates (www.mediate.org) and Mediation Training Institute International (www.mediationworks.com) offer training programs on mediating workplace disputes. These are only a few of the many firms offering such training, so make sure you do your own research to find the program that's right for you.

You can get special training to mediate cases involving individuals with disabilities through the Institute for ADA Mediation at the University of Louisville College of Business and Public Administration in Louisville, Kentucky. Contact the institute at 502-458-9675 or at www.win.net/access.ada.

4. Real Estate

The National Association of Realtors trains association members—realtors, association staff, and attorneys—to mediate disputes that come up in real estate transactions. These include fee splitting between realtors as well as disputes between realtors and clients over fees, services, or property management issues. If you are working in the real estate field and want to mediate, contact the association at 800-874-6500 or at their website at www.realtor.org.

5. Securities

The National Association of Securities Dealers (NASD) trains mediators to resolve disputes between brokers and between brokers and customers. The three-day training programs are held in major cities around the country periodically, but not always regularly—when we checked the site, for example, there were no trainings scheduled. For information, contact the NASD's mediation program office at 212-858-3915 or through their website at www.nasdadr.com.

6. Online Mediation

Online mediation is a relatively new field, using Internet technology to bring parties and mediators together for virtual mediation sessions. One example is SquareTrade, which mediates disputes over purchases on eBay and other online auction and sales sites. Most online programs require mediators to take training specific to the program; the training includes not only mediation skills but also use of the relevant technology and special issues related to the virtual world. Some online mediation groups require that you have already completed a basic mediator training course before enrolling in their specialized training; others will accept you without prior training. Either way, we still recommend you get basic training and some experience before moving into a specialty area.

You'll find more about online mediation as a career field in Chapter 5.

F. Degree Programs in Dispute Resolution

An increasing number of schools are offering conflict resolution curriculum as part of their undergraduate programs. Some offer minors in the field or degrees in interdisciplinary fields, pairing conflict resolution with education, psychology, or business; some have "certificate" programs in conflict resolution that go along with degree programs in other fields. Other schools offer bachelor's degrees in conflict resolution alone. Graduate education in conflict resolution is even more readily available. The list of schools offering graduate programs is growing rapidly.

Appendix E provides a list of graduate and undergraduate degree programs. Take a look if you are interested in pursuing formal education in conflict resolution.

Some programs offer Master of Arts and some Master of Science degrees, and some have doctoral programs. Most conflict resolution programs aren't limited to mediation, but focus more broadly on theories of conflict and the many ways of dealing with it. However, mediation is definitely a centerpiece of most curricula.

Programs can be one, two, or three years long. Some will require residency on campus, but more and more schools offer distance learning options—usually, you'll be required to be on campus for a limited period of time, and spend the rest of your time studying and training through interactive programs by mail or over the Internet. Tuition and fees vary widely, often based on whether you live in the state where the program is offered.

For many students in these programs, mediation or conflict resolution is a midcareer field. Some come to the program to enhance the skills that they need for their current jobs in private business or government. Others are looking to work in conflict resolution organizations, either domestically or internationally, or to teach conflict resolution. And some want to establish a private mediation practice.

Typical course offerings in a conflict resolution program might be:

- theories of conflict
- cross-cultural differences in dispute resolution
- negotiation
- mediation theory and mediation skills (beginning and advanced)
- research methods
- communication skills
- group decision making—theory and practice
- marketing
- training
- clinical or internship programs.

Some schools emphasize practical skills and career preparation as much as theory. If your intention is to become a professional mediator, you'll want to make sure you find a program with that focus—the more theoretically based programs will work better for someone who intends to become an administrator or educator.

So is it worth the time and tuition to get an advanced degree in dispute resolution? It depends. Now that conflict resolution is so widely known and accepted that it is taught in elementary school, you can literally start as a peer mediator in third grade and go on to get a bachelor's, master's, and doctorate. This is a big change from what has historically been a field that people entered from another profession, like law, human resources, or psychology. Many mediators feel that their real-world experience is one of the greatest assets they bring to the table—along with the wisdom of advancing age, perhaps. On the other hand, a mediator who has been steeped in the concepts of conflict resolution from a young age and received significant formal training in the field would also have a lot to offer. Personally, if we were choosing someone to mediate a case, we wouldn't favor a particular mediator simply because he or she had a degree, nor rate a mediator lower for the lack of one.

The major down side for most people considering graduate education in this area will be money—an advanced degree in conflict resolution, like any other graduate education, is very expensive. But it is really a very personal decision, and you'll have to factor in the issue of money along with time, interest in formal education, and future plans. For example, if you are already in the mediation field, either as a practitioner or in a support capacity, getting a degree to improve your theoretical knowledge and to learn advanced skills might enhance both your technique and marketability. Similarly, if you are in midcareer in a related field—human resources, for example—a conflict resolution degree might earn you a promotion or help you make a shift to a mediation-related career. And certainly, if your aim is to teach, do research, or work for a domestic or international organization involved in conflict resolution, such as the Carter Center or the United Nations, then a degree makes perfect sense.

The more programs there are and the more accepted mediation is in the mainstream culture, the more important a degree will become. At the same time, if you're just entering the field with the intention to practice mediation, we offer the same advice we gave at the beginning of the chapter—it might be best for you to invest in some basic training and do a bit of mediation so that you can make an informed decision about whether mediation is for you. Then, if you still have a commitment to the field, consider your educational options and decide whether a degree program makes sense. ●

Job Opportunities in Mediation

We spent considerable time in the previous chapter on the need for high-quality training followed by some experience, even as a volunteer. Once that's completed, you're ready to look for a job or start your own practice. In this chapter, we'll consider jobs that require you to actually mediate. (We'll refer to the same categories of mediation services discussed in Chapter 3, so if you're just dipping in here, you may want to pause and read that chapter first to understand the various services.) If you're interested in mediation support jobs like case management or administration, or in mediation-related jobs like teaching or training, you'll find that information in Chapter 6.

Whatever kind of mediation you want to do, this chapter will give you the information you need to decide where and how to practice—and some particulars about availability of jobs, salary ranges, and mediation career resources.

A. Working for Community Mediation Centers

The 500 to 600 nonprofit community mediation centers around the country rely almost exclusively on volunteer mediators. People volunteer, as we've noted, because community mediation centers offer inexpensive basic training and the opportunity to mediate a variety of interesting cases.

A few centers pay their mediators a small stipend, maybe $25 per case. A center that takes child custody case referrals from the local family court might pay mediators with special training in this area a higher stipend, perhaps $100 a case. One center we know of pays $50 to arbitrators in small commercial cases. Other centers pay nothing to mediators under any circumstances—sometimes, you're lucky to get your parking ticket validated.

Clearly, you're not going to make a living mediating at a community mediation center. Nevertheless, don't overlook volunteering as a good way to start networking your way into the field—and toward a paying job. "People get jobs because their skills become known to their colleagues," advises Craig Coletta, coordinator for the National Association for Community Mediation. "One of the best ways to get a job in the mediation field is to volunteer at a community mediation center in your area and meet other people working in the field." Community mediation centers are also good places to find entry level positions in mediation support, a topic we'll examine further in Chapter 7.

Looking for a local community mediation center? To find a community mediation center where you live, check the phone directory under "mediation" or visit the National Association for Community Mediation's website (www.nafcm.org), where you will find contact information for hundreds of centers nationwide.

B. Court-Connected Mediation Programs

Most states have court-connected mediation programs to help parties resolve civil (noncriminal) cases, such as those involving contracts, consumer claims, personal injuries, and divorces. (For more about these programs, see Chapter 3.)

The best opportunities for mediators in court-connected programs are in state courts that employ their own full-time salaried mediators to handle divorce cases. For example, all California courts have mandatory custody mediation programs in their family courts. Mediators who work for the California court program often have advanced degrees in the social sciences and are required to have professional background in mental health or family counseling. They also must take advanced mediator training through the court. Full-time positions carry salaries ranging from about $45,000 to $75,000, depending on the geographic location.

Job Description

Superior Court Mediator/Investigator

Position: Mediator/Investigator

Organization: Superior Court in Northern California county

Job description: Interview and negotiate with lawyers, litigants, and minors to try to settle custody and visitation disputes; mediate parenting plans to reduce conflict between divorcing parents; make recommendations to the court about custody, visitation, and further proceedings; confer with judges, mental health workers, teachers, and law enforcement where appropriate to assist in developing recommendations; administer data; work with staff on improving mediation, counseling, and investigative skills; speak before groups about program's goals, policies, and procedures.

Requirements: Different depending on job level (I, II, or III), but all include completion of a Master's degree in psychology, social work, marriage, family, and child counseling, or related field and eligibility for licensure with state as a clinical social worker or marriage and famiy therapist; for higher levels experience in those fields is required.

Salary: $40,000–$61,000 depending on job level

Full-time salaried positions are more the exception than the rule. Court-connected programs in most states refer cases to contract mediators, offering only part-time work. Compensation varies by state and even by county, as well as by case type. Some states pay mediators very little or use volunteer mediators; others pay reasonably well.

To get referrals through a court-connected program, you'll most likely have to show that you have adequate training and experience. You may be required to complete a special court-approved training program, depending on how much training you already have. Some states require mediators working in court-connected programs to be lawyers. In Florida, for example, where more than 5,000 certified mediators handle civil cases in the court-connected program, nonlawyers can only handle cases valued at $15,000 or less; all the larger cases are reserved for lawyer-mediators.

Other states permit nonlawyers to mediate but may require them to have more training than lawyer-mediators. In North Carolina, for example, certification is available to lawyers as well as nonlawyers, but nonlawyers must complete an additional six hours of training on court procedures and common legal issues arising in civil cases. They must also provide letters of reference as to their good character, among other requirements.

Once they have been certified for court programs, mediators typically put their names on a list, and either the court assigns them cases on a rotating basis or the parties choose a mediator from the list. It can sometimes be tough for nonlawyer mediators to get chosen. Even if the parties themselves don't care whether the mediator is a lawyer or not, their attorneys often do and steer them toward selecting a lawyer-mediator.

In courts where the parties or judges are free to select any mediator they want from a court's roster, a small number of popular mediators tend to be picked frequently, and the rest hear relatively few cases. In other words, it can be frustrating to put in the effort to make sure you qualify for court-connected programs, only to find that there's not much return in terms of cases coming your way. But even where compensation is slight and the work only occasional, we still encourage aspiring mediators to participate in court-connected programs. It offers opportunities to develop skills, meet other professionals, and let the community know that you are available as a mediator.

Want more information on court-connected mediation? To learn whether your state has a court-connected mediation program and how you can get involved, contact the local clerk of the court. Nolo's website (www.nolo.com) has directories of federal, state, and local courts in each state. You can also contact the National Center for State Courts in Williamsburg, Virginia, which maintains information about court-connected mediation programs nationwide. Call the center at 800-616-6164 or visit their website at www.ncsconline.org. Follow the site map to the alternative dispute resolution section and the mediation subsection, where an NCSC document provides links to the court-connected programs of every state. Another source for information on court-connected ADR is the website of the Center for Analysis of Alternative Dispute Resolution Systems (CAADRS) at www.caadrs.org.

C. Government Mediation Programs

The federal government has an active alternative dispute resolution program that affects many departments and agencies, and the feds are a significant source of jobs for mediators. Government agency use of ADR is required or encouraged, depending on the agency or department, under the Administrative Dispute Resolution Act of 1996.

Overview: Federal Agency ADR

The Department of Justice administers a program called the Interagency Alternative Dispute Resolution Working Group, which, according to its website, was established to "coordinate, promote, and facilitate the effective use of ADR in government." Agencies must report annually on their use of mediation and other forms of alternative dispute resolution. The most recent report concludes that "ADR does a better, quicker, and more cost-effective job than traditional adversarial processes in resolving disputes that involve the public." The report describes ADR programs in all the branches of government, and details cost and time savings in agencies like the Federal Energy Regulatory Commission, the Department of Health and Human Services, the Environmental Protection Agency, the Air Force, and the U.S. Postal Service, whose mediation program is discussed in detail below.

For a list of ADR coordinators at each federal department and agency, including contact information, visit the U.S. Department of Justice website at www.usdoj.gov/odr and follow the prompts to "Interagency Working Group" and then to "Federal Agency ADR Contacts."

In this section, we'll look at some of the agencies that are most active in hiring or contracting with mediators to handle cases arising under federal programs.

1. Federal Mediation and Conciliation Service

Created by Congress in 1947 as an independent agency to promote stable labor-management relations, the Federal Mediation and Conciliation Service (FMCS) mediates contract disputes between employers and unions in the private and government sectors. The FMCS also mediates disputes within government agencies and between agencies and the public, and trains personnel at other agencies to set up their own dispute resolution systems.

Currently, the FMCS employs about 120 full-time mediators who work either at the agency's Washington, DC, headquarters or at the more than 70 field offices throughout the country. Mediators handle labor cases but may also be "loaned" to other federal agencies to handle cases of other types, such as internal claims of employment discrimination.

The sample notice below shows salary and qualification requirements typical for these types of mediator positions. The initials GS, for Government Service, are part of the standard designation for pay scales in federal government jobs.

Job Description

Sample Job Description:
Federal Mediation and Conciliation Service Mediator

Organization: Federal Mediation and Conciliation Service

Title: Mediator

Qualifications: Substantial full-time experience in a leadership role, acquired over a period of several years in the negotiation of collective bargaining agreements. Candidates who fall short of these requirements but have other relevant experience in negotiating or administering collective bargaining agreements may be considered for developmental positions at the GS-9 or GS-11 levels at the agency's larger field offices, where mentoring with an experienced mediator is available.

Salary: Starting GS-12 ($55,958–$61,315); potential to GS-14 ($74,335–$96,637) (salary range is dependent on geographic location, not experience)

For more information about job opportunities at the FMCS, contact the agency at its Washington, DC, headquarters at 202-606-8100 or its website at www.fmcs.gov.

2. Equal Employment Opportunity Commission

The Equal Employment Opportunity Commission (EEOC) enforces the federal Civil Rights Act of 1964 (commonly referred to as Title VII), which prohibits workplace discrimination based on race, sex, national origin, color, or religion. The EEOC also enforces the Equal Pay Act, the Age Discrimination in Employment Act, and the Americans with Disabilities Act.

The EEOC Mediation Program by the Numbers

The EEOC was one of the first federal agencies to establish a mediation program, starting with pilots in four cities in 1991 and launching a national program in 1999. Since 2000, the mediation program has been used in all of the agency's district offices, each of which has its own mediation coordinator. In 2003, the agency conducted over 11,000 mediations, with a resolution rate close to 70%. The agency's own statistics estimate that the monetary benefit of these mediations (including time and money saved) is more than $115 million. And still, only about a third of the EEOC complaints that are filed go through the mediation program, which is voluntary for both employees and employers. Obviously, there's room for a lot of growth, and for a lot of job opportunities for mediators in the future.

The EEOC's mediation program is administered primarily through its 25 district offices, which together employ over 100 mediators. This number includes the ADR coordinators at each district office, plus full-time "internal" mediators distributed among the offices. EEOC offices also contract with hundreds of outside mediators who are trained in mediation and in the laws enforced by the agency.

Minimum qualifications for an EEOC staff mediator generally include five years of experience in negotiation and facilitation and three to five years working with the EEOC, including one year of mediation experience. Staff members generally mediate two to three cases per week and spend the rest of their time doing scheduling and other administrative work related to the cases.

District offices maintain rosters of nonstaff mediators, who are selected based on their backgrounds in employment discrimination law and their training and experience as mediators. About 75% are attorneys, and the rest are either involved in human resources or work full-time as mediators. Pay rates vary by geographic region. (There's a profile in Chapter 3 of one external mediator who works through the San Francisco office.)

Some government agencies now have internal mediation programs for dealing with discrimination claims before they go to the EEOC or after they've been filed. For example, the U.S. Postal Service (USPS) has an internal mediation system called REDRESS (Resolve Employee Disputes, Reach Equitable Solutions Swiftly). More than 10,000 USPS cases are mediated every year. To handle this volume of cases, the postal service primarily depends on outside mediators who work for the program under contract.

To become certified by the agency to mediate these cases, prospective mediators take REDRESS-sponsored training. More than 3,000 mediators are already trained and on the postal service's mediation roster; as this book went to press, the agency had closed the list and was not accepting new mediators. For more information on this program and to stay updated on opportunities, contact the national REDRESS office at 202-268-3991 or check the website at www.usps.com/redress.

3. Other Federal Agencies

Other full-time mediator jobs are scattered throughout the federal bureaucracy. Those with well-established mediation programs include the following:

- **National Mediation Board (NMB).** This agency works to avert strikes involving railroads, airlines, and other forms of transportation. The NMB employs full-time mediators, but not a large number, and extensive background in transportation and labor relations is required. For more information, contact the agency at 1301 K St. NW, Suite 250, Washington, DC 20005, on the Web at www.nmb.gov.
- **Community Relations Service.** This agency, which is part of the U.S. Department of Justice, helps local communities resolve racial and ethnic conflicts. Staff trained in mediation are stationed in ten regional and four field offices across the country and are available on a 24-hour basis. For more information, visit the agency's website at www.usdoj.gov/crs.
- **National Association of Securities Dealers (NASD).** NASD is a private corporation regulated by the Securities and Exchange Commission (SEC). NASD has a dispute resolution program to help resolve disputes between investors and their brokerage firms. You don't need specific experience in the securities industry to be included on NASD's nationwide roster of approved mediators, but parties are more likely to choose a mediator who knows the laws and practices of the industry. Mediators are paid directly by the parties at a rate that is set by the NASD. For information about the NASD program and to find out whether the program is accepting new mediators, check the website at www.nasdadr.com.

- **Medicare Mediation Program.** The federal Medicare program has a new mediation program through which Medicare beneficiaries can mediate concerns about quality of care with their doctors or other health care providers. Right now, the program is only in the pilot stages, but as it grows, more mediators will be trained to conduct these sessions. The pay depends on the geographic area but is generally around $100 per hour, plus expenses. Nonlawyer mediators are very welcome in this program. You can find information about the program by calling 800-841-1602 or checking the Web at www.lumetra.com.

Want more information on mediation opportunities with the federal government? Go to the U.S. government's official website for employment information, www.usajobs.opm.gov. The site, maintained by the Office of Personnel Management, posts vacancy listings for all federal agencies and provides detailed information on how to apply for jobs. To find openings for mediators on this website, try searching under "mediator," "conciliation specialist," or "alternative dispute resolution."

D. State and Local Government Programs

State government mediation programs offer mediators opportunities for full-time, part-time, or contract employment.

Most states now have, or are in the process of forming, special offices to coordinate mediation services throughout the state. Some offices are sponsored or partly funded by state governments; others are independent, nonprofit organizations that assume this role themselves. A good way to learn about job opportunities in your state is by contacting the statewide mediation office. You'll find a list of these offices in Appendix D.

Examples of State Government Mediation Programs

In Massachusetts, the state Department of Education employs mediators to handle disputes involving special education programs, and the Office of the Attorney General runs a program involving peer mediation in the schools. A statewide Office of Dispute Resolution maintains a panel of some 60 mediators (mostly private practitioners) who have contracts with other state agencies to hear cases involving housing, land use, state policy, and other matters.

In Oregon, a new state commission is training mediators to handle disputes involving people with disabilities. If planned funding is available, the mediators will be paid between $50 and $200 an hour. The Oregon Commission on Dispute Resolution coordinates ADR programs throughout the state and maintains a roster of mediators in the private sector who are available to serve in state-run mediation programs.

Most local bar associations have dispute resolution sections, and most have mediator referral services. Generally, the referral services will be limited to lawyer-mediators, but some section meetings are open to nonlawyer members, and might be a good source of both education and networking opportunities. And lots of school districts have mediation programs, so even cold calls to district administrators to find out how they hire mediators might get you some interesting information.

E. Private Dispute Resolution Companies

Many private companies providing alternative dispute resolution services offer job opportunities for mediators. At the high end, if you're an experienced mediator, particularly one with a legal background, you can become an active, independent contractor with a large, national ADR firm or even more than one. If that's not your profile, you can join the panel of smaller, local ADR firms and hope they do enough business to call you to hear cases. Online dispute resolution is another area where private mediators can find cases. In this section, we'll consider these various job opportunities.

I. Judicial Arbitration and Mediation Service (JAMS)

The largest private, for-profit ADR firm is JAMS (formerly Judicial Arbitration & Mediation Service), headquartered in Irvine, California, with 22 regional dispute resolution centers nationwide. JAMS aims for the market segment that includes complex commercial disputes, including real estate, construction, business, and serious personal injury.

JAMS by the Numbers

"JAMS is known for high-stakes, multiparty, and complex cases, and its mediators are the cream of the crop," notes JAMS national communications manager Michele Apostolos. JAMS handles about 10,000 cases per year, about 70% of which are mediation cases. The company has over 200 neutrals, all of whom are full-time and exclusive with the company, meaning they don't work for any other ADR firm.

Almost all of JAMS's neutrals are retired judges or attorneys. The panel also includes a former White House counsel and U.S. congressperson, several retired federal judges, and retired state supreme court justices

JAMS mediators work as independent contractors and share a portion of the fees they bring in to the company. Their time is charged to the parties at rates of $350 an hour and higher. Depending on how in-demand they are as mediators and how complex their cases are, JAMS mediators earn from $150,000 to more than $1 million a year, making them among the highest-paid mediators in the country.

For most people reading this book, working with JAMS is probably an unlikely career path. The exception is if you are an established, experienced lawyer with some mediation experience and a strong reputation in a particular area of law. But if you are a new mediator, one of the smaller national or local ADR firms will be a more realistic place for you to look for opportunities.

The JAMS Foundation offers special opportunities for mediators of color. The JAMS Foundation, a nonprofit foundation established by the company, provides financial assistance for conflict resolution initiatives for the benefit of the public interest. In 2003, the foundation, in cooperation with the American Bar Association's Dispute Resolution Section, launched a program called "ACCESS ADR." The program will offer training, mentoring, and business development support to experienced mediators from underrepresented racial and ethnic groups. For more information, check the JAMS Foundation website, www.jamsfoundation.org, or contact the JAMS Foundation at 800-448-1660.

You can learn more about JAMS on the Web at www.jamsadr.com or by calling 949-224-1810.

2. American Arbitration Association

The American Arbitration Association (AAA), founded more than 75 years ago, has expanded—despite its arbitration-focused name—to include mediation. Although it handles the same types of complex commercial cases as JAMS and other for-profit ADR firms, AAA distinguishes itself from other providers by its not-for-profit status, and focuses on education and public service in addition to providing direct ADR services.

AAA by the Numbers

AAA has a competitive advantage—it is the ADR provider identified in thousands of employment, insurance, construction, and general commercial contracts. This means that the parties to these contracts must use AAA to mediate contract disputes. As a result, its caseload is massive: the AAA administered 174,000 cases in 2003.

AAA operates 34 offices domestically and one in Dublin, Ireland. The organization has about 8,000 neutrals on its panels, about 1,000 of whom are mediators—the rest do arbitration. "Mediation is something you have to do frequently to stay good at it," explains senior vice president Mark Appel, "so we're selective about who gets on our mediation panel." Some of the mediators practice other professions, such as law, and mediate for AAA only occasionally, but many others are full-time mediators who handle a large volume of cases. Unlike JAMS, AAA does not have exclusive arrangements with its neutrals.

AAA mediators set their own fees, which range from about $125 an hour for less experienced mediators handling smaller cases to about $500 an hour for highly skilled, commercial mediators handling seven-figure disputes. AAA's highest-paid mediator charges $7,500 a day.

Most AAA mediators are lawyers, but there are nonlawyers on the panel, too. Most nonlawyer mediators come from the industry that uses their mediation services—for example, engineers, architects, contractors, or construction managers may mediate disputes in the construction industry.

Becoming an AAA mediator is only slightly more accessible than finding work with JAMS. How do you get to be an AAA mediator? "First, get yourself trained," advises Appel. He recommends getting experience with a community or court-connected program, and spending some time getting familiar with AAA. Once you have a track record, apply to be on the AAA roster. "Generally, we'll want to see that you've done ten to 20 business-to-business or employment cases. Community cases and family disputes won't qualify you."

"Officially, applicants for AAA's mediation panel should have ten years experience," says Appel. "More important than ten years is a track record of success as a mediator. We're not looking for people just out of school, but high-quality mediation experience is more important to us than an arbitrary number of years."

Want to know more about AAA? For more information, contact the corporate headquarters in New York City at 800-778-7879, or visit their website: www.adr.org.

3. Other National Private ADR Firms

There are other mediation firms providing dispute resolution services nationwide.

For example, Resolute Systems, Inc., is headquartered in Milwaukee, Wisconsin. Resolute Systems is a worldwide dispute resolution provider, with five regional offices in the U.S. The company primarily uses attorney-mediators. Resolute Systems also provides training and consulting, and by virtue of its size employs many people in mediation support positions. Resolute Systems also partners with Cybersettle.com, an online dispute resolution service. For more about Resolute Systems, call the headquarters at 800-776-6060 or check online at www.resolutesystems.com.

Another national firm is called just that: National Mediation. With its main offices in Sacramento, California, National Mediation has a roster of some 3,000 mediators nationwide. The company participates in a larger clearinghouse for employee assistance programs, and the majority of the cases that come in for mediation are divorce cases, with workplace, personal injury, and real estate matters rounding out the workload.

National Mediation is one of the only national private ADR firms that include a significant number of nonlawyer mediators on its panels. The company requires that mediators have at least 100 hours of mediation experience; for mediators whose background is solely in community mediation, the requirement is raised to 150 hours. You'll have to provide references from parties you've worked with in mediation and/or other mediators you've worked with who can vouch for your experience and skills. Once you are accepted on the panel, you can set your own fees—but you'll need to be strategic about it. James McPherson, vice president of the company, notes that the mediators who get the most work are those who set their fees reasonably and have experience in areas that are in demand, like family law and personal injury. To learn more about applying to be on a National Mediation roster, contact the company at 800-286-0777 or at www.nationalmediation.com.

4. Local Private ADR Firms

There may also be private ADR firms in your local community. In some areas, like the San Francisco Bay Area, such firms proliferate, with some specializing in particular areas and some in particular types of panelists, like retired judges. Your best bet for finding companies like this in your area is to look in the telephone book or do an Internet search for mediation or ADR in your city or county, and then contact the firms directly for information about hiring practices.

F. Online Dispute Resolution

Opportunities for mediators online are still few and far between, but as the volume of Internet transactions and disputes continues to increase, online mediation work should be more available—and more lucrative. Online mediation generally works in two ways. Internet businesses, especially auction and other sale sites, can use online mediation to resolve disputes about purchases made on the Web. And private dispute resolution companies can use Internet technology to resolve any kind of dispute using a virtual mediation process.

Because of the growth potential in this area, this is a great time for a new mediator to sign up with some online services and develop skills and credentials in online mediation. And because online disputes tend to involve straightforward commercial transactions rather than complex legal cases, online mediation firms do not appear to favor mediators with law backgrounds to the same extent as other private ADR companies—creating more opportunities for nonlawyer mediators.

Resources for Online Mediation Opportunities

There are a lot of online dispute resolution sites, but many of them use computerized "blind bidding" programs to resolve conflicts over money, and don't involve live mediators. Even those sites need administrative workers, though—see Chapter 6 for more about mediation support jobs. A few of the sites that offer live mediators for online mediation—and thus might have opportunities for mediators—are:

- The Better Business Bureau at www.dr.bbb.org
- National Arbitration & Mediation (which incorporates what used to be called clicknsettle.com) at www.namadr.com
- Mediation & Arbitration Resolution Service at www.resolvemydispute.com
- SquareTrade, an online dispute resolution firm devoted solely to disputes over e-commerce, at www.squaretrade.com, and
- www.webmediate.com, an online resolution site for disputes of all kinds.

In addition, the Mediate.com website at www.mediate.com provides a major online presence for all forms of mediation, offers referrals and directories, maintains a library of resources, and develops websites and Internet technology—including technology that can support online mediation—for practitioners and organizations. Jim Melamed, cofounder and chief executive officer of Mediate.com, believes that mediators can benefit from embracing online mediation as a component of their practice. He believes that "in the future, we won't talk so much in terms of face-to-face mediation or of online mediation but of our ability as mediators to best integrate the Internet into our practices. For example, if I'm doing divorce mediation, I can meet with a couple face-to-face several times, but later I can also work with them online at lower cost. Similarly, if I'm mediating a communitywide dispute, I can have an online discussion with literally hundreds of participants."

Familiarity with Internet technology and an ability to conduct mediations in ways other than the traditional face-to-face format can help distinguish you from other mediators. Cultivate these skills if you can.

Case Study

SquareTrade

SquareTrade specializes in resolving disputes arising out of online transactions, such as nondelivery of goods or services, misrepresentation, improper selling practices, guarantees or warranties that aren't honored, unsatisfactory services, credit and billing problems, and unfulfilled contracts. SquareTrade got its start handling disputes from the online auction site eBay, and continues to mediate a significant number of auction-related matters. The service has expanded to include offline disputes, particularly in the area of real estate.

When a dispute is filed, the parties are encouraged to resolve it themselves through direct negotiation, discussing the issues through a password-protected Case Page on the SquareTrade website. If that effort fails, the parties may request a live mediator, who conducts an online mediation through password-protected chat rooms.

SquareTrade mediators are paid according to the type of case and the complexity of it, and the pay can range widely, from $10 or $15 or as high as $100 per hour—or mediators can be paid on a flat per-case basis. In some cases SquareTrade guarantees the mediator a certain number of hours or case volume—so, for example, a guarantee of 20 hours per week mediating, even at $10 an hour, might be desirable. Some cases, such as real estate matters, might involve much higher fees.

Currently, Square Trade has over 250 mediators. In recruiting mediators, the firm looks at experience levels, especially in regard to specialty areas of e-commerce such as intellectual property, employment and service matters, real estate and construction, and general commercial disputes; experience as a neutral, especially internationally; and multilingual skills or cross-cultural expertise. A legal background is not among the listed factors for recruiting mediators, but there might be cases where subject-matter expertise is required.

SquareTrade offers a training program to help mediators learn the special ins and outs of online mediation work. The training is free, but in exchange SquareTrade requires mediators to sign a noncompetition clause—an agreement that they won't mediate with another online company for a year—and a nondisclosure clause, promising not to give out information about SquareTrade's training or its programs.

In the course of training, mediators are assigned five cases under supervision and then evaluated. If the evaluation is positive, they are certified as a SquareTrade mediator.

For more information on being a SquareTrade mediator, visit www.squaretrade.com.

G. Independent Mediators in Private Practice

Having a private mediation practice is the dream of many an aspiring mediator. And that dream can become a reality—although establishing a private practice is not easy, it's energizing and usually rewarding in the end.

With private practice, there are no "job opening" notices to help you get started. At some point, after you get proper training and some mediation experience, you will just have to hang out your shingle and go for it. That means renting an office or setting one up in your home, printing stationery and business cards, getting phone and fax lines and probably a website, opening a separate bank account, buying insurance, setting your fees, and attending to all the other details involved in starting a business.

And then you'll need cases. Most likely, those cases are not going to come to you—at least at first. Instead, you'll have to go out and get them. And in order to do that, you'll have to figure out what makes you different from all the other mediators out there who might want the same cases. You'll need to bring an entrepreneurial spirit to the whole enterprise, learn something about marketing, and get some advice about how to position yourself in the local field. In other words, just being a good mediator isn't enough—especially at first. You have to be a good businessperson, too.

Networking is enormously important. Fortunately, there are lots of opportunities to meet others in the field. You will probably want to join the national Association for Conflict Resolution (ACR), and it's also a good idea to join whatever local mediation organizations exist in your area. ACR has local chapters in most states; even when there's not a local ACR chapter, there may be a mediation group that you can join.

Make Yourself Known

If you have expertise in a particular area, or just an interest in a particular topic, write an article for your local organization's newsletter or for Mediate.com, which publishes articles regularly and offers great exposure. Make presentations at conventions. Most important, get to know other mediators—find out what they do and make sure they know what kinds of cases you take, in case they have a case to refer—or want to call you for advice. Make sure you let other mediators come to know your dedication, capacity, intelligence, and commitment to the field. They will often be your best source of referrals.

Target your networking to the type of practice you want. For example, if you're thinking of developing a practice in workplace mediation, it's not the employees or the company president who will want to bring in a mediator, it's the upper-level management and maybe the human resource director. In divorce mediation, you need to reach mental health professionals, accountants, and of course, divorce lawyers. But you also want to make sure that barbers and beauticians know who you are and what you do—these people know what's happening in their customers' lives, and can steer them toward mediation.

Finally, take advantage of your entire personal and professional network. If you were in software development and now want to go into divorce mediation, contact all the software people you know to let them know about your new line of work. And while you're working on developing your practice, you can pick up some extra experience and income by handling cases through local court-connected or government mediation programs, and through regional or national ADR firms that will accept you onto their panels. Get on as many panels as you can.

As we noted in Chapter 3, mediators in private practice generally engage in one of three types of work: divorce and family mediation, a specialty other than divorce, or general practice. We'll consider each of these next.

1. Divorce and Family Mediation

Perhaps a majority of mediators in private practice are divorce mediators. There is a strong and growing demand for divorce mediation—in some cities more than 25% of divorcing couples mediate their split—and a mediator can build a practice by cultivating a fairly narrow range of referral sources, principally therapists, clergy, and divorce attorneys.

Fees for divorce mediation vary depending on where you work and who uses your services. In a large city, mediators catering mostly to affluent couples may charge upwards of $200 per hour. One mediator in California, whose clientele includes movie stars and media executives, charges $500 an hour. In small towns and rural communities, mediators may be happy to get $75 an hour. Divorce mediators in midsize communities can expect to earn on average about $100 to $150 an hour. Those who offer a sliding fee scale based on ability to pay generally accept around $60 per hour and up.

Although some divorce mediators may be earning six-figure incomes, we think a fair estimate of what full-time mediators make in average-sized cities is somewhere between $50,000 and $100,000 per year. However, many active divorce mediators do not mediate full time—instead, they spend some of their time training new mediators or continuing to practice whatever profession they were in before they became mediators—for example, therapy, law, or social work.

You may wonder whether there is enough demand for divorce mediation in your community to support another mediator; you may be discouraged to see a long list of divorce mediators in your local yellow pages or other directory. The reality is that some of those listings are for folks who don't mediate even ten cases a year. That's not because the market is saturated but because not everyone makes it as a mediator—some are dabbling in mediation while spending most of their time doing something else, and some just don't have the skills, personality, or ambition to build a successful practice. The handful of mediators who are making a living at mediation probably do 75% of the work in town. They're the ones who have both the skills and the marketing savvy to make a go of it—and if you're serious about becoming a divorce mediator and are willing to invest the time and energy to develop a practice, there's no reason you can't join this successful group.

Case Study

Dolly Hinckley

Dolly Hinckley became a divorce mediator in 1984, when the field was still very new. A divorced mother of four, she was employed as property manager at a senior citizen's high-rise in Rochester, New York. For many years, she worked at that job until 1:00 P.M., then mediated in the afternoons. As a nonlawyer, she recalls, "It was an uphill struggle in those days because of resistance from the bar association, but I did a lot of networking with mental health professionals and attorneys, and took a lot of people out to lunch so they'd get to know me and my practice." She gave presentations to many interest groups, such as Equal Rights for Fathers and the American Association of University Women.

Today, Hinckley has a well-established divorce mediation practice in Rochester, New York. She works out of her home in the suburbs, and most of her referrals come from former clients. She continues, however, to network with referral sources and regularly accepts invitations to speak before support groups of people going through separation and divorce.

Hinckley charges on a sliding scale based on income, from $75 to $130 an hour. Each year she completes between 40 and 50 mediations. In addition to divorce, Hinkley does some marriage mediation, such as prenuptial mediation and helping married couples with specific issues; she also mediates disputes among family members and does volunteer mediation at the local community mediation center.

Hinckley estimates that she has about 20 billable hours a week. "Mediating full-time doesn't mean you're mediating nine to five every day," she explains, noting that although she charges for drafting documents, she generally doesn't bill for the time she spends preparing for each session—for example, doing background research on a retirement plan or reviewing relevant laws or court decisions.

Hinckley believes that the demand for divorce mediation will keep increasing. "It's not that the number of divorces is increasing, but more people getting divorced are now looking at mediation first rather than going to attorneys. Years ago, in support groups people used to ask each other, 'Who's your lawyer?' but now it's 'Who's your mediator?'"

Hinckley says she's glad to help new people coming into the field. "I'll help anybody who really wants to be a mediator," she says, "but when I get an initial call from somebody, I don't encourage them because I know it takes a considerable amount of time to get set up and build a profitable practice. Most don't want to give up their day job, but I know from my own experience that it's only when you do quit the day job and put all your energies into mediation that you can become successful. If the person who calls me has already made that decision—to be serious about building a practice—then I'll help them."

There are plenty of resources available to help you get started with a divorce mediation practice. As we discussed in Chapter 4, your first job is to find a divorce mediation trainer approved by the Association for Conflict Resolution—and try to find someone who will help you get started by mentoring you, introducing you to referral sources, and providing forms to use in your practice.

You can also purchase forms and other materials (such as computer programs for case tracking) from private vendors, many of whom advertise in publications and on websites of the major mediation organizations, such as Mediate.com and ACR. ACR itself sells a "Mediation Marketing Toolkit" that includes a marketing video, brochures, audiotapes, and articles about starting and running a practice. Contact ACR at 202-464-9700 or on the Web at www.acrnet.org.

2. Other Specialty Mediators

Divorce is not the only field of specialization for mediators. The advantages of specializing include the opportunity to become expert in one area, which not only can improve the quality of your work but will simplify your life because you don't have to keep up with developments in different fields. Another advantage is that, by specializing, you can narrow the focus of your marketing and better target referral sources. For example, people who specialize in construction mediation can focus their marketing efforts on a clearly defined group of potential clients: attorneys who handle construction litigation; developers, architects, and engineers; claims adjusters at commercial insurers; and major contractors. That's still a lot of people to cultivate as clients, but it's a focused and manageable list.

Another area of specialty that has emerged in recent years is workplace mediation. Federal and state antidiscrimination laws allow employees to file claims for discrimination and wrongful termination. And employers have become more willing to use mediation in these cases, both to avoid potentially expensive lawsuits and to preserve their workforce. In addition, many medium- and large-sized businesses have conflict resolution policies and procedures that call for mediation for interpersonal disputes among employees, to try to avoid discrimination claims—and conflict in the workplace—by mediating at an early stage. If this is something that interests you as a specialty, you'll want to get special training, and to cultivate as referral sources human resource officers, middle managers at major corporations, and lawyers who specialize in employment cases.

Real estate is also a fertile area for mediators. If you are a real estate agent or broker shifting to a mediation career, you might find a specialty in helping to mediate post-sale disputes about failures to disclose, or disputes between property co-owners about use or renovation of the property.

Use What You Know

If you're thinking of developing a specialty practice, consider whether you are already in a field that would lend itself to a mediation practice. For example, if you are a civil engineer, construction mediation might be the natural area in which to specialize. If you are a teacher, education and school-based mediation would be a logical specialty. And lawyers looking to shift from an advocacy practice into mediation often specialize in the same types of cases they argued as litigators.

3. General Mediators

Among the most satisfying types of mediation practice, but perhaps the toughest to establish, is a general practice in which you handle cases in a variety of subject areas. In the early days of mediation—in the 1980s and 1990s—it would have been nearly impossible for even the most skilled mediator to make a living as a general practitioner. Outside of a few specialty areas like insurance or construction, awareness of mediation wasn't widespread enough for people to refer enough cases to a general mediator. Fortunately, that has changed for the better, and today it is possible, though still difficult, to make a living as a general mediator. In fact, some very able, energetic, and ambitious people are doing it right now.

A general practice will vary, of course, according to what the local market offers as well as the mediator's background, interests, and skills, and the needs of the local market. Successful independent practitioners, however, do have a few things in common. First, they practice in large communities where the market is large enough to sustain their business. Second, they are good at promoting themselves and their practices by writing articles, speaking, teaching, tending their websites, and so on. Third, they are very, very busy—if they're not mediating cases, they are soliciting new ones. But they love it. That's why they do it and why they succeed.

Case Study

Moshe Cohen and The Negotiating Table

Moshe Cohen conducts his general mediation practice, which he calls The Negotiating Table, in Cambridge, Massachusetts. Cohen, who holds a bachelor's degree in physics and a master's degree in engineering, as well as an M.B.A., worked 12 years in engineering and project management before making a career change in 1995 and becoming a mediator.

"As someone with a general mediation practice," he says, "I have to build a house out of a whole lot of little bricks. I do a little of this and a little of that. To be successful in this way, you have to have a long-term view and keep at it. I've been at it for nine years, and only in the last two years has it become a self-sustaining business and a reliable source of income."

In the past nine years, Cohen estimates he's done more than 300 mediations. Early on, while he continued his work as an engineer, Cohen did almost all his cases pro bono (without a fee). Many of these cases (he estimates more than 150) were referred to him through a court-connected program. "I did those pro bono cases," he explains, "because coming into this field without having the natural marketing outlet that being an attorney would have given me, my entree to the field was experience, and the quickest way to get experience was through pro bono."

Once he gained experience, however, he still needed paying clients. "As a nonlawyer in this field," he says, "you face tremendous challenges. People don't go to mediation on their own; they go to their attorney who then has a strong bias in favor of attorneys when they select a mediator."

To overcome this hurdle, Cohen focused on the business community. "All these other attorney-mediators are connected to the legal community in ways I'm never going to be, but a lot of business people don't like lawyers and are glad to use a businessperson as a mediator if they know one." To develop his contacts with people in business, Cohen writes a regular column on negotiation and conflict management for a weekly Boston business newspaper, gives presentations to area business groups, and spends a great deal of time meeting with potential clients. "There was a period for about a year," he recalls, "when I never had breakfast at home. I was always going to some sort of chamber of commerce breakfast or other networking group to meet people and make connections."

Many of Cohen's cases involve some kind of business dispute. These include contract cases, partnership dissolutions, and employment disputes between companies and employees. He also mediates securities cases through the panel of the National Association of Securities Dealers, employment cases through the U.S. Postal Service, and employment discrimination cases through the EEOC.

Case Study, cont.

Moshe Cohen and The Negotiating Table (continued)

Cohen does some divorce mediation, but not much. "I don't particularly like doing divorce mediation, and it's hard to keep up with it without doing it full-time, so often I bring in a comediator to help me. But then I end up making less money at it."

Cohen's standard fee is $200 per hour. His practice has grown progressively over the years—but in year seven, business took a sharp leap upward and has continued growing in the two years since then.

The Negotiating Table also offers corporate training, which he describes as "a lucrative part of the practice." He regularly presents workshops to businesses on negotiation and mediation and teaches a course on negotiation in the M.B.A. program at Boston University.

For more information about The Negotiating Table, contact Moshe Cohen at 617-577-0101, or visit the website at www.negotiatingtable.com.

Nonlawyers, take heart. We know that this chapter might seem somewhat discouraging to mediators who are not lawyers—and there is no question that lawyers have an advantage in trying to establish themselves as mediators. But if you are a nonlawyer mediator, remember that the largest national ADR organization, AAA, does use nonlawyers as mediators, including engineers, architects, building contractors, and construction managers—and so does National Mediation, another nationwide private dispute resolution provider. There are also lots of smaller private ADR firms with nonlawyer mediators on their panels, especially social workers and therapists in the area of divorce mediation. If you are not a lawyer, you will need to really use your expertise in whatever field you've worked in to distinguish yourself—and you'll need to make sure you get excellent training and significant experience before looking for work in the field. For nonlawyers, associating yourself with an experienced, established mediator is the best thing you can do, so cultivate your relationships with care.

Want more information on starting a private practice? If you decide to start a private practice as a mediator, check out *Mediation Career Guide*, by Forrest Mosten (Jossey-Bass). And don't forget that you are opening a small business—find resources that will help you be successful. Nolo has a multitude of books for small business owners, including books on writing a business plan, leasing space, forming a corporation, and the legal aspects of starting and running a small business. For more information on these books, check out Nolo's website at www.nolo.com.

Career Resources

The following is just a partial list of resources that will help you get an idea of the types of jobs that are available, or, if you are ready, help you search for work as a mediator. In addition to any of these sites, don't neglect to check for mediator jobs at any large institution you can think of—if there's a school district, a big medical facility, or a large employer in your community that you might have interest in working for, go to that entity's website and search for mediation jobs.

- www.crinfo.com is a clearinghouse website that includes individual job postings as well as a listing of other sites with dispute resolution job postings.
- You can find job listings at www.mediate.com by clicking on "Forums" and then on "Employment Opportunities." You'll have to register, but registration is free.
- The National Association for Community Mediation lists dispute resolution and administrative positions in the area of community mediation. The website is at www.nafcm.org.
- The Fresno Pacific University Center for Peacemaking and Conflict Studies website has job listings across the country and around the world at www.peace.fresno.edu.
- The Professional Mediation Association lists job opportunities on its website at www.promediation.com.
- For students interested in dispute resolution careers, an interesting site is www.campus-adr.org. Click on the "student center" link and follow the links to find career information.

Job Opportunities in Mediation Support

Most of us mediators would love to spend all our time mediating—and some get to do just that. But for many, the market isn't quite there yet. The good news, however, is that there are lots of jobs that *support* the practice of mediation. Unless a mediator works entirely alone, he or she is going to be part of an organization—and from the most humble community mediation center to the largest private ADR company, all mediation services need some people to create and implement programs and manage the office, and others to go out and drum up business. These positions are essential to the mediation field and many actually pay better than mediating.

Peter's own experience bears this out. Over the years, he's worked not only as a mediator but as a program director at a community mediation center, a sales representative and case manager at private mediation firms, and a trainer—all satisfying jobs because of their strong connection to conflict resolution.

So if you don't have the opportunity to work in a paid position as a mediator, or if you like the idea of mediation but know that your personality and skills are better suited to a support role, this chapter will help you identify some of the opportunities available in mediation support. We'll consider jobs in management and sales, including administration, case management, and sales and development. (Chapter 7 looks at mediation-related jobs, like ombuds work, teaching and training, and facilitation.)

Unlike some of the mediator jobs we looked at in the previous chapter, in which lawyers sometimes have an advantage, jobs in mediation support truly are open to all. For many of these jobs it's actually an advantage to have a background in something other than law, such as management, sales, or teaching.

A. Administration

Running a mediation service is a challenging task. You're dealing with clients, all of whom are involved in conflict and are usually anxious about the process as well as the outcome. You're coordinating the schedules of dozens of mediators with differing skill levels, backgrounds, areas of expertise, and expectations for income. And you must provide physical space for secure and quiet sessions, all the while adhering to the rules of mediation and the laws of confidentiality. If you're in the private sector, you have to invoice quickly and accurately not just one client but always at least two and sometimes half a dozen, depending on the number of parties in a case.

Challenging it may be, but if you do it well, you'll have the satisfaction of knowing you made it possible not only for people to resolve hundreds of disputes a year, but also for the mediators themselves to do their work in a safe, efficient, and pleasant environment. All in all, you'll have helped in a tangible way to create a more peaceful and civil community.

1. Community Mediation

Just as nonprofit community mediation centers are an excellent place to start out as a mediator, they also offer good entry-level positions in administration. As we've noted, there are hundreds of centers nationwide; in some states, each county or district has its own center. Most centers have an executive director to manage the center's fiscal operations, including budgeting and grants administration. The executive director also manages the staff, oversees volunteer mediators and interns, and, if time and skills permit, mediates cases. At some centers, the executive director is the only paid staff member; at others the center might employ case managers, development (fundraising) staff, volunteer coordinators, and administrative personnel.

Job Description

Executive Director

All the sample job descriptions in this chapter are excerpted from actual ads posted on the Internet in the six months before this book was published. We've tried to provide examples that are fairly typical for each position in terms of the job description, required background, and salary.

Here's a sample ad for an executive director, excerpted from an ad posted on the Internet by a center in Seattle.

Position: Executive Director

Organization: Nonprofit community mediation center in the Pacific Northwest

Job description: Full-time position reporting to the board of directors. The E.D., along with the board and staff, develops the vision and policies that guide the organization; manages staff; ensures the organization has good financial management practices; develops funding resources; manages administrative reporting responsibilities; networks with courts, social service organizations, and governmental agencies; and is the public face of the organization.

Requirements: Five years management experience in nonprofit, public, or private social services organizations, or equivalent education and experience; ability to do strategic planning, fundraising, team-building, administration, and networking. Desirable qualifications include prior experience working with a board, and mediator certification.

Salary: Begins at $44,000

As you can see, salaries for community mediation center executive directors are relatively modest. This job is in a medium-sized city, and centers in big cities might pay considerably more, while those in more rural areas would pay significantly less. No matter where they are located, community mediation centers are nonprofits and the pay reflects that. The relatively low pay for these jobs tends to create a high turnover, as people work for the nonprofits a few years and then move to higher-paying positions in government or the private sector. In the opinion of Craig Coletta, coordinator for the National Association for Community Mediation, this creates "a brain drain at community mediation centers"—a problem his organization and others are working to mitigate by seeking funding to increase pay scales for community mediation center staff.

The good news, however, is that the high turnover makes these administrative positions available on a regular basis.

2. Government and Court-Connected Programs

Salaries for government administrators are more competitive. We examined government programs in Chapter 5, among them the mediation program run by the EEOC. As an example of the background, duties, and salary of an administrator of a government mediation program, consider the following profile of Loretta Feller, ADR coordinator for the EEOC's Cleveland district office.

Profile: ADR Coordinator

Name: Loretta Feller

Title: ADR coordinator

Mediation Service: EEOC District Office, Cleveland, Ohio; also serves on board of Mediation Association of Northeast Ohio, of which she is a founding member and past president

Educational Background: Master's in public administration with a specialty in human resources; bilingual in English and Spanish

Years in This Position: Eight

Previous Position: Supervisor, EEOC investigations

Duties: Supervises three staff mediators and support staff; recruits and supervises 45 external mediators; mediates about 20 cases herself a year out of annual office caseload of about 400 cases.

Salary: $79,858–$103,818 (GS-14)

Satisfactions of the Job: "People say, 'Don't make a federal case out of it,' but when they come to EEOC, they've already made it a federal case. I get a lot of satisfaction seeing them resolve these matters by crafting a solution that meets their needs. When I started, I was kind of taken aback by the expressions of gratitude I received. The parties would come up and pump my hand and say 'Thank you, thank you.' Better yet, occasionally they actually reconcile, and come to understand each other better."

The National Mediation Board recently ran a vacancy announcement for a more entry-level position as a "mediation assistant." The pay range was from GS-07 to GS-09—meaning the salary could be anywhere from $33,431 to $53,165.

Many state governments also run mediation programs, including court-connected mediation programs. These programs also offer opportunities for jobs in administration.

Job Description

Sample Job Description: Mediation Liaison (Court Program)

This is another entry-level position, in a court-connected community mediation program in an East Coast city.

Position: Mediation Liaison

Organization: Jointly administered by state's attorney and local community mediation program

Job description: Part-time position working in a courthouse, screening criminal cases for referral to community mediation program, and developing cases for community mediation center staff; some involvement in training participants, attorneys, and state's attorney staff in mediation.

Requirements: Entry-level position

Salary: $14/hr, 12-16 hours per week

Similar administrative positions are available with local mediation programs and international organizations. Here are a few more examples of recently posted job openings that are representative of openings in the field (if salaries aren't listed, it's because they weren't listed in the job posting).

- **Regional Director** for a nonprofit mediation center approved by the state office of dispute resolution in the Midwest. Responsible for operating regional dispute resolution office, providing direct services, training, administration, and program development. Salary $21,000–$27,000 plus benefits.
- **Executive Director** of nonprofit mediation center providing mediation services to local small claims and family courts. Responsible for managing and overseeing staff, developing funding, managing training, and promoting ADR locally and statewide.
- **Family Court Program Director** at nonprofit mediation center providing mediation services to local family court. Responsibilities include supervising mediation programs, including scheduling and outreach, recruiting and training mediators, networking with community and social programs, and administering required statistical information. Master's or law degree preferred.

- **Mediation Center Project Coordinator,** Restorative Justice Schools Project. Project coordinator will work with students, administrators, parents, and community members to design and implement restorative justice programs in local schools. Full-time position.

B. Case Management

In our view, one of the most interesting support positions—and possibly the one that most calls for mediation skills even though you're not officially mediating—is case management (or case development, as it's sometimes also called). Every mediation service uses case managers—the people who have the first contact with prospective disputants and who gently and skillfully shepherd the parties to the mediation table.

When a disputant calls a private, governmental, or nonprofit mediation center, the case manager takes information from that party and explains what mediation is, how it works, what it costs, and so on. Then, typically, the case manager contacts the other party to try to get an agreement to mediate. Often the second party is ignorant of mediation and suspicious of any service the first party contacted. The skilled case manager, however, can educate and reassure that party to the point where an initial "no" to mediation becomes a "yes." Often the reluctant party ends up thanking the case manager for persisting in getting both sides to the table.

The skills a good case manager needs include patience, a talent for communication, the ability to be neutral and project neutrality—and did we mention patience? Getting the parties to the table can sometimes be almost as challenging as mediating—and can involve a similar process of listening, reflecting back, and discussing options.

Case managers may also be responsible for helping the parties select a mediator, scheduling the session, generating needed paperwork, getting fee deposits, and generally making sure the process runs smoothly and professionally.

Job Description

Case Manager

Organization: Nonprofit community dispute resolution center in Northern California

Job description: Full-time bilingual (Spanish) case manager for family programs. Responsibilities include client intake, case development and case management for disputants; assigning mediators to each case; scheduling mediation; supporting volunteer mediators; ensuring appropriate follow-up contact; preparing reports on case data.

Requirements: Qualified candidate must be bilingual in Spanish and English, have skills and experience with families in conflict, and have excellent communication skills and proven organizational skills. Mediation experience desirable but not required.

Salary: $38,000–$44,000, depending on skills and experience; health and other benefits provided

Sometimes you might find a case manager position called by a different name, such as administrative assistant. And a dispute resolution service that offers arbitration services as well as mediation is required to meet certain legal requirements when taking in cases, and might refer to a job that is essentially one of case management as a "legal assistant" position. A job that included an arbitration component would add some additional administrative tasks to the usual case manager's job description, including sending out hearing notices and making sure paperwork complies with legal requirements.

Private ADR companies, including online mediation providers, also use case managers. For example, JAMS has between 50 and 70 case managers nationwide, about one for every two or three mediators.

"Case managers are vital to the professional and neutral administration of the resolution process," says Michele Apostolos, JAMS national communication manager. "Case managers are the point of contact for the parties, often explaining the range of ADR formats available, bringing the parties together to agree on who the neutral will be, and the location, date, and time of the session. They receive a good deal of training and are known for being service- and detail-oriented."

Case managers can earn anywhere from about $20,000 at community mediation centers in nonurban areas to $70,000 at the large private dispute resolution providers in big cities. Like mediators, case managers come from all kinds of backgrounds—but they all tend to qualify as the proverbial "people person," to be comfortable with lots of work on the telephone, and, as noted above, to have good communication skills and lots of patience.

C. Sales and Development

If there are no cases coming into a mediation office, there is nothing for mediators to mediate. Someone has to be out in the community looking for cases. This holds true for nonprofit mediation services as well as private ADR companies. If you are skilled in sales or marketing, the mediation field offers plenty of opportunities.

In the private sector, most ADR companies employ several salespeople to call on businesses or agencies that can refer cases for mediation or arbitration. Typically, referral sources include insurance companies, court administrators, law and human resource departments in major corporations, and law firms.

Case Study

Sales

Co-author Peter Lovenheim describes his experience selling his private ADR company at the beginning: "When I started, I spent most of the first year driving among several cities in our region, giving hour-long presentations to groups of adjusters at insurance company claims offices. I'd explain how mediation could help resolve claims for personal injury and property damage, show a video of a typical mediation session, and then explain how to submit cases to our company for what we hoped would be rapid and successful resolution through mediation or arbitration. On the way home, I'd stop at a couple of law firms and try to get a few minutes with the head of the litigation department to make a similar pitch. More than half the insurance companies referred cases to us, often within weeks or a couple of months; responses from law firms were about the same, although the referrals tended to be much slower, often taking many months or even years."

Some ADR companies pay their salespeople a salary; others pay on commission, based on business generated.

An unusual aspect of sales in the mediation field is that sometimes a firm's sales rep must sell not only the idea of mediation but also the actual mediators.

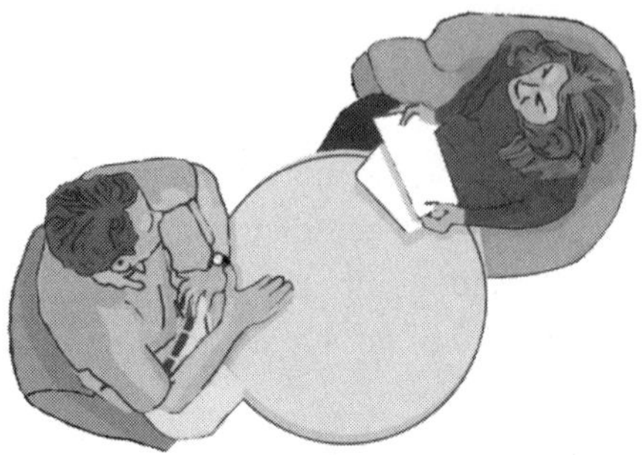

When parties select a mediation service, particularly for large, complex cases involving significant amounts of money, they often choose a mediation service based on the particular mediators available on that company's roster. Therefore, companies that handle major cases often promote themselves by promoting the individual mediators on their panels.

For example, at each of its major offices, JAMS employs a special kind of salesperson it calls a practice development manager. This person's job is to increase business by helping the company's mediators present themselves effectively to businesses and law firms that might refer cases to the company.

Salaries for JAMS practice development managers are in the range of $60,000 to $75,000—and higher in large cities like New York and San Francisco.

Nonprofit mediation centers also rely on marketing to get the word out in the community about the availability of their services. The marketer's task is to call on judges, court clerks, prosecutors, and community groups like neighborhood associations to encourage them to refer cases. This type of job, which might be called something like "community relations specialist," would likely pay in the $20,000 to $25,000 range in a small community and more in larger cities and with larger agencies.

The nonprofit mediation world also must rely on fundraising, in what sometimes can seem an endless process of seeking financial support. At the local level, community mediation centers typically employ a development director whose job it is to keep money flowing in through grants, donations, and special events. Typically, funding sources include local and state government agencies, broad-based charities such as United Way, and private foundations and individuals. Many community mediation centers rely primarily on grant funding for their budget. Fundraising activities are ongoing, including regular mailings to solicit support and special events such as award dinners.

Job Description

Development Director

Position: Director of Development

Organization: National mediation organization based on the East Coast

Job description: Full-time position managing development and execution of development plans to meet funding needs of the organization. Responsibilities include developing a fundraising plan, planning and executing an annual campaign, developing grant funding sources, establishing relationships with private donors, and coordinating development activities of executive director, board, and staff.

Requirements: B.A. and five years experience in field of development; ability to manage staff; good communication skills

Salary: $40,000–$45,000

Available positions in sales and development can be found on the various mediation websites listed at the end of Chapter 5, but if you have a background either in sales or development and want to work in mediation, we suggest you start by just calling any local, regional, or national firm in which you're interested. Find out whether they have sales or development employees, and emphasize that you have the necessary background in those fields, as well as knowledge about the mediation process. They might be very glad to find someone with that combination of skills and experience.

D. Service

For some people reading this book, it's just not going to be possible to pursue a career in mediation or mediation support. If that's true for you, you can still participate in the field in meaningful ways by contributing your time or money. Check out Chapter 7, Section E, for more about this. ●

Job Opportunities in Mediation-Related Fields

In addition to mediation support work, there are also careers in what we will call "mediation-related" fields. Many of the same values that lead people to become mediators—a desire to ease conflict, encourage positive communication, and empower people to resolve disputes—can also lead to great job satisfaction in one of these mediation-related positions.

A. Careers as an Ombudsperson

Mediators who are interested in using their dispute resolution skills for something other than classic mediation might want to consider working as an ombudsperson—a neutral investigator of complaints and conflict in the public and private sectors. ("Ombudsman" is a commonly used term for this position, but we prefer "ombudsperson" for its gender neutrality.)

An ombudsperson might work for a private company, a government agency, or any other type of organization where conflict might arise—which, of course, is every organization. Lots of health care organizations use ombudspeople to investigate and help resolve problems and conflicts, both within the organization and between the organization and its patients or other consumers. Many other types of private companies also have ombudspeople who deal with complaints against the company or conflict among employees. Government organizations also sometimes use ombudspeople in positions that are created by legislation, in which the ombudsperson is authorized to report findings and recommendations to government officials. And most colleges and universities have an ombuds office to deal with complaints from students, faculty, and staff.

A mediator already has many of the skills that are necessary to be an effective and successful ombudsperson, and with some additional training can add ombuds work to his or her repertoire. Most ombudspeople use a number of mediation skills in their jobs—for example, active listening, reframing, identifying underlying interests, and creative problem solving. Although some actually facilitate discussions between disputants, for the most part an ombudsperson works with one party at a time. The goal of the work is to conduct a fair and complete review of the complaint and make recommendations to the organization about how best to resolve the problem.

Often, the ombudsperson's recommendations will affect many more people than just the individual who made the original complaint, because they may result in policy changes or other systemic changes in how the organization operates.

1. Ombuds Training

Just as mediators can get experience working as volunteers in community and court-connected programs, there are similar opportunities for those who want to get initial training and experience in ombuds work. For example, the U.S. Navy administers a volunteer program, and there are numerous ombuds programs in the field of long-term care. For training opportunities, see "Resource List: Training and Job Opportunities for Ombudspersons," below.

2. Ombuds Jobs

In the United States alone, there are hundreds of established ombuds programs—in private industry, government, education, and health care.

If you're considering ombuds work, it's important that you have a working knowledge of the industry or sector where you want to work. The deeper your understanding of the corporate culture in the field, and/or of the operations of the specific organization, the more credibility you'll have in your job search and, ultimately, in your job. This is another area where using what you already know can get you a big advantage—if you spent years in health care or working for a large corporation, you'll have an advantage in looking for ombuds jobs. In contrast, if you don't have a strong background in a particular field, simply having mediation skills may not get you very far in trying for ombuds work.

A sample job description for a long-term care ombudsperson is shown below. The salary is $32,500, which is about par for the course for a government agency. Ombudspeople in other fields can make much more, with salaries often averaging between $70,000 and $90,000, and those working in private industries may earn salaries as high as $175,000.

Job Description

Ombudsperson

Here's a sample ad for an ombudsperson, excerpted from an ad posted on the Internet by a long-term care administrator in Seattle.

Position: Long-Term Care Ombudsman

Organization: County agency

Job description: Full-time position resolving complaints from residents of long-term care facilities, mediating, documenting cases, and assisting with information and complaint phone line

Requirements: B.A.; two years advocacy experience with one year in social services, or combination of education and experience

Salary: $32,500

Resource List: Training and Job Opportunities for Ombudspersons

There are a number of organizations that provide training and ongoing continuing education opportunities, including local and national conferences at which you can meet and network with established ombudspeople from around the country. Most of these resources also offer job listings for ombudsperson positions.

- The Ombudsman Association at www.ombuds-toa.org
- The United States Ombudsman Association at www.usombudsman.org
- The University & College Ombudsman Association at www.ucoa.org
- The ombudsperson section of the Association for Conflict Resolution (ACR) at www.acrnet.org
- The ombudsman committee of the American Bar Association (ABA) at www.abanet.org/adminlaw/ombuds
- The National Long-Term Care Ombudsman Resource Center at www.ltcombudsman.org
- The International Ombudsman Institute at www.law.ualberta.ca/centres/ioi.

B. Facilitation

Facilitation is another field that uses many of the same skills as mediation—with the added requirement that you must be comfortable working with large groups of people and dealing with issues that are sometimes open-ended. Facilitators work with groups of varying sizes and in various ways—from a single brief meeting to a series of meetings or a multiday retreat.

It's very common for nonprofit agencies and private companies to use facilitators for board and staff retreats, to help with team building, developing or refining the organization's mission, strategic planning, decision making, or problem solving. Problem solving is the area in which a facilitator might use mediation-related skills the most—to help an organization deal with interpersonal conflicts, low employee morale, or other workplace problems. The facilitator does many of the same things a mediator does, like gather information about the problem and help the people involved talk with each other and reach an understanding and a plan for going forward.

Facilitators often work with companies and agencies that have regular board meetings, using an outside facilitator to make sure that the meeting stays on track and that every board member is participating. Facilitators can also help with community meetings where issues important to the local community are discussed. Sometimes, meetings like this are arranged through a community mediation center, and the center's mediators are called upon to facilitate. There are also opportunities for facilitators to help with meetings when government agencies and/or private companies are required by law or by contract to hear from the local community about the impact of a particular project they're planning.

Many facilitators work in private practice, either alone or with a small group. But some work for corporations, managing meetings full time as in-house facilitators and trainers. And many people facilitate meetings as part of their regular jobs in administration or human resources.

Resource List: Training and Job Opportunities for Facilitators

Here are a few websites that provide information and job listings for facilitators:

- International Association of Facilitators at www.iaf-world.org.
- Interaction Associates at www.interactionassociates.com is probably the largest private facilitation trainer in the U.S., offering beginning and advanced facilitation training
- National Organizational Development Network at www.odnetwork.org (for more about organizational development, see Section D1, below)
- There's a very active facilitators' online listserv sponsored by the Center for Policy Research at the University of Albany, at www.albany.edu/cpr/gf.
- There may also be local facilitators' organizations in your area. Check the International Association of Facilitators website for links to regional and local organizations.

C. Training and Teaching

In this book, we'll distinguish training and teaching by including in our definition of training any kind of instruction done outside a college or university, and defining teaching as providing instruction within a college or university. Many mediators make training or teaching a minor component of their practice as a way to pick up some extra income and to meet a lot of people, some of whom might later refer cases. Other mediators find that they enjoy training or teaching so much—and they are so good at it—that training becomes their primary work, and they end up mediating only on the side.

1. Mediation and Related Training

If you think you might be interested in training, don't think that your work would be limited just to individuals who think they might want to become full-time mediators. A mediation trainer might work with lots of different individuals and groups—for example:

- civil court judges interested in referring cases to mediation
- police and district attorneys who refer cases to mediation or who want to learn mediation skills to help them in interventions with citizens

- midlevel corporate managers who want to learn how to resolve disputes between employees
- attorneys or therapists who want to become mediators, or who simply want to understand mediation in order to recommend it to their clients
- middle-school students who have been selected to act as peer mediators
- retired judges about to join the panel of a private ADR firm, or
- teenage counselors at a summer camp seeking skills to resolve disputes that might arise among themselves or their campers.

Some community mediation centers use their own employees to train volunteer mediators. Often a center also develops its own programs to train local business and professional groups in basic conflict resolution, as well as to teach local students participating in peer mediation programs. Salaries for full-time trainers at community mediation centers could be anywhere in the range of $25,000 to $50,000 at centers in midsized cities—and there are not that many full-time opportunities; many centers use outside trainers on a contract basis.

Private mediation training firms offer significantly higher salaries than community mediation centers. For example, a firm like CDR Associates, a national conflict resolution training organization based in Boulder, Colorado, might pay in the range of $50,000 per year.

Job Description

Sample Job Description: Mediation Trainer

This job description is excerpted from a posting from a nonprofit conflict resolution center in the Midwest.

Position: Associate Director in Charge of Training

Organization: Nonprofit conflict resolution organization

Job description: Full-time position as lead trainer. Responsibilities include coordinating and scheduling all trainings, recruiting trainers, serving as lead trainer, creating and implementing a long-range training plan and increasing revenue from training services, marketing training services, creating and revising training materials, assisting executive director with operational issues

Requirements: College degree and mediation and training experience

Salary: $35,000–$50,000 depending on experience

If you prefer to work on your own rather than with an organization, you can set up on your own as an independent trainer. One independent trainer we know developed a nice part-time practice doing peer mediation training in the local schools, charging $50 to $75 an hour for a 12-hour program. Trainers who specialize in divorce mediation generally charge $1,000 and up for a basic 40-hour training course. Other trainers specialize in industrial relations, delivering the message of conflict resolution to corporate managers dealing with workplace conflicts. These trainers can earn about $2,000 for a one- or two-day training course for midlevel managers.

In addition to training folks in mediation, if you know something about another topic that is of interest to mediators you can offer continuing education classes. For example, a mediator or facilitator might offer training in communication skills, dealing with difficult people, a particular mediation style or method, or even a topic like tax issues for small business owners (which might interest mediators in private practice).

Also, if you want to become a trainer in topics unrelated to mediation or communication, there are lots of opportunities in the human resources field for training in the corporate world. Not to belabor the point, but again, if you already have expertise, you might be able to parlay it into a training career.

Obviously, before you can launch a career as a mediation trainer, you'll need to get trained yourself and get some solid experience mediating. You'll then want to take advanced training to further develop your skills. The more training you take, the better trainer you're likely to become. In addition, the people you learn from may become good contacts in the field and help you develop your own career as a trainer.

Need more information about training? For information about conflict resolution training, the website at www.peaceeducation.com offers information about training for trainers in the education context, and links to other organizations. Another site, www.trainingforum.com, lists opportunities for trainers' training. You can also check out the website of the American Society for Training and Development, which is primarily dedicated to workplace trainers but does have lots of information about the field in general, along with interesting links.

One of the best ways to learn about training is to watch the people who train you. If you haven't even begun your mediation training yet, then you have a great opportunity right from the beginning to observe the techniques of whomever you choose to train you in mediation skills. Consider what worked for you and what didn't, what seemed to work or not work for others, whether the day went quickly or seemed to drag, how the trainers dealt with different learning styles or with conflict in the room, and whatever else strikes you as important about the trainers' methods. This will be just as valuable as taking a class in the theory of learning, and will give you a head start on thinking about whether you might want to consider training as a career option or a sideline to mediation.

2. Teaching and Academic Administration

As more people seek to become mediators, there is an increasing demand not only for trainers but also for teachers and professors of conflict resolution. The demand is evident from elementary, middle, and high schools right up through college and graduate programs. If you love the idea of mediation but your strength is in academics, becoming a teacher of conflict resolution may offer you a satisfying career. In an important way, you will also help advance the entire field of mediation: some of the people you train may go on to found new ADR companies, government mediation programs, or nonprofit organizations that promote conflict resolution, thus creating jobs for even more mediators in the future—as well as contributing to creating peace.

As we discussed in Chapter 4, dozens of colleges and universities today offer master's and doctoral programs in conflict resolution. Many others offer individual courses and certificate programs. This creates a new, strong demand for teachers.

Job Description

Sample Job Description: Director of Mediation Services

This job description is excerpted from a posting from a large university on the West Coast.

Position: Director of Mediation Services

Organization: Public university mediation program dealing with campus and community conflicts and training

Job description: Full-time position as director of mediation services. Responsibilities include managing all aspects of the mediation program including mediations, marketing, education, and liaison with campus committees, departments, unions, and staff.

Requirements: Mediation experience and experience with marketing, outreach, and supervision; understanding of different mediation methods

Salary: $60,000–$107,000 depending on experience and qualifications

If your strength is in teaching, there has never been a better time to pursue an academic career in conflict resolution. Many academicians combine their teaching with actual mediation, sometimes finding a niche for themselves on the panels of private ADR companies or (more likely) helping set up and oversee mediation systems to resolve disputes within the university community. Others consult with officials in government and industry, advising on how to apply theories of conflict resolution to actual public policy disputes.

Job Description

Sample Job Description: Assistant Professor

This job description is excerpted from a posting from a private college in the South.

Position: Assistant Professor of Conflict Resolution

Organization: Private university Justice Studies program

Job description: Teach core courses in justice studies; develop courses in the area of conflict resolution and analysis

Requirements: College degree; background in communication and interest in teaching issues related to family, gender, and community conflict resolution desirable

Salary: Information not available

Need more information about academic job opportunities? For information on colleges and universities that may offer teaching positions in their conflict resolution programs, see the discussion of academic programs in Chapter 4 and check out Appendix E.

D. Conflict Resolution Consulting and Coaching

Like facilitation and training, the fields of conflict resolution consulting and coaching are related to mediation in the skills they require. Conflict resolution consultants and coaches use listening, skillful questioning, and interest-based problem solving to help individuals and organizations succeed at their goals. Although the two fields are related, they're not the same, and we'll treat them separately.

1. Consulting

Of course, there are many types of consultants—you can probably find consultants in almost every line of work. And like experts in any field, people with mediation training sometimes consult in the area of dispute resolution.

A conflict resolution consultant works with organizations to develop dispute resolution policies and procedures, and might also consult on developing curriculum for conflict resolution training. Most mediators with good training and a measure of experience can offer consultations as well as mediation sessions—but you won't get that kind of business unless you advertise yourself that way. You'll also have to do some networking with the types of organizations that might use dispute resolution consulting services. Fees for consulting are generally about the same as for mediation, ranging anywhere from $75 to $250 per hour.

Need more information on consulting? To learn more about consulting, take a look at *Flawless Consulting*, by Peter Brock (Jossey-Bass). It's not about conflict resolution consulting specifically, but it will give you a good sense of what consultants do. You can also check out *Getting Started in Consulting*, by Alan Weiss (John Wiley & Sons).

A consultant might also help a nonprofit or private company figure out whether its organizational structure is causing problems between employees or other conflicts, and design a new structure. This kind of consulting, often called "organizational development," is a whole consulting field unto itself. Most companies seeking to work with an organizational development consultant will look for someone with training from a college or university program in the field. To learn about organizational development training and career options, check out the National Organizational Development Network at www.odnetwork.org.

2. Coaching

Coaching is another fast-growing field in which mediation skills can be put to use. Like consulting, coaching is a job that can be done in many different fields. In fact, probably the fastest-growing area of coaching is called "personal" or "life" coaching, in which the coach works with an individual client on setting and achieving personal and professional goals. Certainly, mediation skills would benefit you if that's a direction you want to take. But as a mediator, you might be even more suited to coaching people who have a dispute, because it allows you more involvement in the actual resolution of conflict.

If you are considering becoming a mediator, you probably believe that you have the personal qualities we discussed in Chapter 2, such as good listening skills, patience and perseverance, and the ability to read other people. These are some of the same qualities you'll need if you're considering a coaching career.

The main difference in terms of the process is that as a coach, you won't sit down with people in a room to help them work out a solution to a dispute they are having. Instead, you'll work with one of the parties individually, coaching him or her on communication skills, so that any dispute resolution process that takes place can be as effective as possible. You might coach a supervisor, for example, on how to help two employees who are in conflict. Or you might work with someone who is a party in a mediation with another mediator, helping him or her prepare to communicate positions and interests as effectively as possible.

In essence, you are supporting people in solving their own disputes, and modeling and advising on good communication skills, just as you do as a mediator—but in a different format.

Want more information about coaching? For information about coaching careers, and training to become a coach, check out the International Coach Federation website at www.coachfederation.org, as well as www.coachinc.com, and www.coachville.com.

E. Some Final Words of Encouragement

Chapters 6 and 7 are intended to make sure that you know how many opportunities there are for you to use the skills that you will develop as you become a mediator. We are very much aware that mediation is not the easiest career path you could choose, and that a good deal of patience and dedication will probably be required to get you where you want to be—but we encourage you to make the investment to get there.

And if for some reason you choose not to pursue a day job as a mediator or in a mediation support or mediation-related field, we encourage you to incorporate the skills and philosophy of mediation into your life in other ways. For example, even if you're not going to mediate for pay, there's no reason you can't still volunteer as a mediator at your local community center. Most folks who mediate at those centers are not professional mediators, in fact—just people who want to make a contribution by helping to resolve conflict close to home.

Also, each of the hundreds of community mediation centers operating across the county has a board of directors that oversees their operations and helps guide their growth. Serving as a board member of your local center can be a wonderful way to make a positive contribution to the peaceful future of your community. And if you are able, you can contribute financially to your local community mediation center, to national research efforts aimed at improving the delivery of mediation services, to a college that wants to establish a program in conflict resolution (or already has one), or to a local middle school that would set up a peer mediation program if only it had the funds to hire staff to run it.

In other words, if you think that mediation is a good thing, there's a lot you can do to promote and support it. And that includes taking your mediation skills home and incorporating them into your relationships with the people you love. Use them to help create what the Bible calls *shalom bayit*—peace in the house. Your family, your community, and all those who strive for peace, will thank you for it. ●

Sample Rules of Mediation

This set of mediation rules is used by Empire Mediation & Arbitration, Inc., a private dispute resolution company in Rochester, New York. These rules are typical of those used at mediation services that handle a variety of types of cases.

Mediation Defined/Role of the Mediator: Mediation is a voluntary process in which the parties to the dispute meet together confidentially with a neutral third party called a mediator. The mediator does not take sides and has no authority to make a decision, but works with the parties to help them evaluate their goals and options in order to find a solution to the dispute that is satisfactory to all sides.

Initiating the Process: Any party to a dispute may begin mediation by sending a completed Submission Form to Empire Mediation & Arbitration, Inc. ("Empire").

Agreement to Mediate: After receiving the Submission Form, Empire will contact all parties to a dispute to determine their willingness to participate in mediation. If the parties agree to participate, each will sign an "Agreement to Mediate" before the first mediation session begins.

Appointment of Mediator: From its panel of mediators, Empire will propose to the parties the names of one or more mediators qualified and available to mediate their case. The panelist will be chosen by agreement of all the parties.

Scheduling/Notice of Mediation: Empire will schedule the mediation at a time and place convenient to all parties, and notify the parties in writing of the date, time, and location of the session. The mediation may be rescheduled upon a party's request but a rescheduling fee will be assessed against the requesting party.

Representation at Session: Each party must be represented at the mediation by a person with authority to settle the dispute. Individuals may be represented by legal counsel, and counsel are encouraged to have their clients participate. Insurance companies may be represented by claims staff or defense counsel. Other business corporations may be represented by executive staff or counsel. It is not necessary for witnesses to attend the mediation, but if they do, their testimony will be heard at the mediator's discretion.

Rules of Evidence: The rules of evidence common to judicial and arbitral proceedings do not apply in mediation. Any statement, document, or other record offered by the parties will be admissible unless the mediator, in his or her sole discretion, finds it irrelevant or otherwise inappropriate in the session.

Session Procedure—Opening Statements: The mediator will begin the session with an opening statement in which he or she will explain the purposes and procedures of the session. The parties will then make their opening statements, explaining their positions on the issues in dispute, including the presentation of any documents, photographs, and oral or written summaries of witness testimony that would be helpful to the mediator in understanding the case.

Session Procedure—Private Caucuses: During the mediation, the mediator may meet in private caucus with each of the parties and counsel, to explore positions and settlement options. Any information disclosed to the mediator in the caucus will be kept confidential unless the party expressly tells the mediator it may be disclosed to the other parties.

Confidentiality: The mediation session constitutes a settlement negotiation and statements made during the mediation by the parties are inadmissible, to the extent defined by law, in subsequent judicial or arbitral proceedings relating to the dispute. The parties will maintain the confidentiality of the mediation and not introduce as evidence in any future arbitral or judicial proceeding statements made by the mediator or by any other party, or subpoena the mediator to testify or produce records in any such proceeding. Evidence otherwise discoverable or admissible is not made inadmissible or nondiscoverable because of its use in mediation.

No Record: No stenographic or other record of the mediation will be made.

Conclusion of the Mediation: The mediation will conclude when the parties have reached a settlement agreement, or upon the oral or written request of the parties, or at the discretion of the mediator.

Settlement Documents: If a settlement agreement is reached during the mediation, the parties will make their own arrangements for the drafting and later execution of settlement documents.

Exclusion of Liability: Mediators conducting sessions for Empire act as independent contractors; they are not employees of the company. Neither the mediators nor the company act as legal counsel for any of the parties in the dispute. Parties have the right to legal counsel and are encouraged to obtain legal advice in connection with a dispute. Parties not represented by counsel at a mediation may condition a settlement agreement upon review by their attorney.

Neither mediators nor the company are necessary parties in judicial proceedings relating to mediation, and neither the mediator nor the company will be liable to any party for an act or omission in connection with a mediation conducted under these rules.

Standards of Conduct for Mediators

These standards were developed by three professional groups: the American Arbitration Association, the American Bar Association, and the Society of Professionals in Dispute Resolution (now merged into the Association for Conflict Resolution). The Standards are intended to apply to all types of mediation, but in some cases their application may be affected by laws or contractual agreements. The standards reproduced here were finalized in 1994. The committee is currently working on revisions, and is soliciting comments at the dispute resolution section of the ABA website, www.abanet.org/dispute.

I. Self-Determination: A Mediator Shall Recognize That Mediation Is Based on the Principle of Self-Determination by the Parties.

Self-determination is the fundamental principle of mediation. It requires that the mediation process rely upon the ability of the parties to reach a voluntary, uncoerced agreement. Any party may withdraw from mediation at any time.

COMMENTS: The mediator may provide information about the process, raise issues, and help parties explore options. The primary role of the mediator is to facilitate a voluntary resolution of a dispute. Parties shall be given the opportunity to consider all proposed options. A mediator cannot personally ensure that each party has made a fully informed choice to reach a particular agreement, but it is a good practice for the mediator to make the parties aware of the importance of consulting other professionals, where appropriate, to help them make informed decisions.

II. Impartiality: A Mediator Shall Conduct the Mediation in an Impartial Manner.

The concept of mediator impartiality is central to the mediation process. A mediator shall mediate only those matters in which she or he can remain impartial and evenhanded. If at any time the mediator is unable to conduct the process in an impartial manner, the mediator is obligated to withdraw.

COMMENTS: A mediator shall avoid conduct that gives the appearance of partiality toward one of the parties. The quality of the mediation process is enhanced when the parties have confidence in the impartiality of the mediator.

When mediators are appointed by a court or institution, the appointing agency shall make reasonable efforts to ensure that mediators serve impartially.

A mediator should guard against partiality or prejudice based on the parties' personal characteristics, background, or performance at the mediation.

III. Conflicts of Interest: A Mediator Shall Disclose All Actual and Potential Conflicts of Interest Reasonably Known to the Mediator. After Disclosure, the Mediator Shall Decline to Mediate Unless All Parties Choose to Retain the Mediator. The Need to Protect Against Conflicts of Interest Also Governs Conduct That Occurs During and After the Mediation.

A conflict of interest is a dealing or relationship that might create an impression of possible bias. The basic approach to questions of conflict of interest is consistent with the concept of self-determination. The mediator has a responsibility to disclose all actual and potential conflicts that are reasonably known to the mediator and could reasonably be seen as raising a question about impartiality.

If all parties agree to mediate after being informed of conflicts, the mediator may proceed with the mediation. If, however, the conflict of interest casts serious doubt on the integrity of the process, the mediator shall decline to proceed.

A mediator must avoid the appearance of conflict of interest both during and after the mediation. Without the consent of all parties, a mediator shall not subsequently establish a professional relationship with one of the parties in a related matter, or in an unrelated matter under circumstances which would raise legitimate questions about the integrity of the mediation process.

COMMENTS: A mediator shall avoid conflicts of interest in recommending the services of other professionals. A mediator may make reference to professional referral services or associations which maintain rosters of qualified professionals.

Potential conflicts of interest may arise between administrators of mediation programs and mediators and there may be strong pressures on the mediator to settle a particular case or cases. The mediator's commitment must be to the parties and the process. Pressures from outside of the mediation process should never influence the mediator to coerce parties to settle.

IV. Competence: A Mediator Shall Mediate Only When the Mediator Has the Necessary Qualifications to Satisfy the Reasonable Expectations of the Parties.

Any person may be selected as a mediator, provided that the parties are satisfied with the mediator's qualifications. Training and experience in mediation, however, are often necessary for effective mediation. A person who offers herself or himself as available to serve as a mediator gives parties and the public the expectation that she or he has the competency to mediate effectively. In court-connected or other forms of mandated mediation, it is essential that mediators assigned to the parties have the requisite training and experience.

COMMENTS: Mediators should have available for the parties information regarding their relevant training, education, and experience. The requirements for appearing on a list of mediators must be made public and available to interested persons. When mediators are appointed by a court or institution, the appointing agency shall make reasonable efforts to ensure that each mediator is qualified for the particular mediation.

V. Confidentiality: A Mediator Shall Maintain the Reasonable Expectations of the Parties With Regard to Confidentiality.

The reasonable expectations of the parties with regard to confidentiality shall be met by the mediator. The parties' expectations of confidentiality depend on the circumstances of the mediation and any agreements they may make. A mediator shall not disclose any matter that a party expects to be confidential unless given permission by all parties or unless required by law or other public policy.

COMMENTS: The parties may make their own rules with respect to confidentiality, or the accepted practice of an individual mediator or institution may dictate a particular set of expectations. Since the parties' expectations regarding confidentiality are important, the mediator should discuss these expectations with the parties.

If the mediator holds private sessions with a party, the nature of these sessions with regard to confidentiality should be discussed prior to undertaking such sessions.

In order to protect the integrity of the mediation, a mediator should avoid communicating information about how the parties acted in the mediation process, the merits of the case, or settlement offers. The mediator may report, if required, whether parties appeared at a scheduled mediation.

Where the parties have agreed that all or a portion of the information disclosed during a mediation is confidential, the parties' agreement should be respected by the mediator.

Confidentiality should not be construed to limit or prohibit the effective monitoring, research, or evaluation of mediation programs by responsible persons. Under appropriate circumstances, researchers may be permitted to obtain access to statistical data and, with the permission of the parties, to individual case files, observations of live mediations, and interviews with participants.

VI. Quality of the Process: A Mediator Shall Conduct the Mediation Fairly, Diligently, and in a Manner Consistent With the Principle of Self-Determination by the Parties.

A mediator shall work to ensure a quality process and to encourage mutual respect among the parties. A quality process requires a commitment by the mediator to diligence and procedural fairness. There should be adequate opportunity for each party in the mediation to participate in the discussions. The parties decide when and under what conditions they will reach an agreement or terminate a mediation.

COMMENTS: A mediator may agree to mediate only when he or she is prepared to commit the attention essential to an effective mediation.

Mediators should only accept cases when they can satisfy the reasonable expectations of the parties concerning the timing of the process. A mediator should not allow a mediation to be unduly delayed by the parties or their representatives.

The presence or absence of persons at a mediation depends on the agreement of the parties and mediator. The parties and mediator may agree that others may be excluded from particular sessions or from the entire mediation process.

The primary purpose of a mediator is to facilitate the parties' voluntary agreement. This role differs substantially from other professional-client relationships. Mixing the role of a mediator and the role of a professional advising a client is problematic, and mediators must strive to distinguish between the roles. A mediator should therefore refrain from providing professional advice. Where appropriate, a mediator should recommend that parties seek outside professional advice, or consider resolving their dispute through arbitration, counseling, neutral evaluation, or other processes. A mediator who undertakes, at the request of the parties, an additional dispute resolution role in the same matter assumes increased responsibilities and obligations that may be governed by the standards of other professions.

A mediator shall withdraw from a mediation when incapable of serving or when unable to remain impartial.

A mediator shall withdraw from the mediation or postpone a session if the mediation is being used to further illegal conduct, or if a party is unable to participate due to drug, alcohol, or other physical or mental incapacity.

Mediators should not permit their behavior in the mediation process to be guided by a desire for a high settlement rate.

VII. Advertising and Solicitation: A Mediator Shall Be Truthful in Advertising and Solicitation for Mediation.

Advertising or any other communication with the public concerning services offered or regarding the education, training, and expertise of the mediator shall be truthful. Mediators shall refrain from promises and guarantees of results.

COMMENTS: It is imperative that communication with the public educate and instill confidence in the process. In an advertisement or other communication to the public, a mediator may make reference to meeting state, national, or private organization qualifications only if the entity referred to has a procedure for qualifying mediators and the mediator has been duly granted the requisite status.

VIII. Fees: A Mediator Shall Fully Disclose and Explain the Basis of Compensation, Fees, and Charges to the Parties.

The parties should be provided sufficient information about fees at the outset of a mediation to determine if they wish to retain the services of a mediator. If a mediator charges fees, the fees shall be reasonable considering, among other things, the mediation service, the type and complexity of the matter, the expertise of the mediator, the time required, and the rates customary in the community. The better practice in reaching an understanding about fees is to set down the arrangements in a written agreement.

COMMENTS: A mediator who withdraws from a mediation should return any unearned fee to the parties. A mediator should not enter into a fee agreement which is contingent upon the result of the mediation or amount of the settlement. Comediators who share a fee should hold to standards of reasonableness in determining the allocation of fees.

A mediator should not accept a fee for referral of a matter to another mediator or to any other person.

IX. Obligations to the Mediation Process.

Mediators have a duty to improve the practice of mediation.

COMMENTS: Mediators are regarded as knowledgeable in the process of mediation. They have an obligation to use their knowledge to help educate the public about mediation; to make mediation accessible to those who would like to use it; to correct abuses; and to improve their professional skills and abilities.

APPENDIX C

National and Regional Mediation Organizations and Services

Organizations listed below can be contacted for more information about the mediation field in general, such as career and training opportunities, state and federal legislation, and references to specific mediators or mediation services in your area.

The mediation services listed include private dispute resolution companies as well as nonprofit associations that provide mediation, arbitration, and other dispute resolution services for actual cases.

MEDIATION ORGANIZATIONS

Academy of Family Mediators
4 Militia Drive
Lexington, MA 02173
617-674-2663
Provides support, training, and guidance for practicing divorce and family mediators, and information for the public, including a list of approved training programs and mediators who have met requirements for Academy membership.

American Bar Association
Section on Dispute Resolution
740 15th St., NW, 8th Floor
Washington, DC 20005
202-662-1680
Monitors and provides information on dispute resolution and the courts, and dispute resolution legislation pending and enacted.

Association of Family and Conciliation Courts
329 West Wilson Street
Madison, WI 53703
608-251-4001
Monitors and provides information on court-sponsored divorce and family mediation and arbitration programs.

Conflict Resolution Center International
2205 East Carson St.
Pittsburgh, PA 15203
412-481-5559
Provides information to individuals and communities working to resolve neighborhood disputes, and racial, ethnic, and religious conflicts.

CPR Institute for Dispute Resolution
366 Madison Avenue, 14th Floor
New York, NY 10017
212-949-6490
Encourages large businesses and law firms to use mediation and other dispute resolution techniques as a first resort to settle disputes.

National Association for Community Mediation
1726 M St., Suite 500
Washington, DC 20036
202-467-6226
Supports the growth of nonprofit, community mediation centers. Can provide contact information for hundreds of centers nationally.

National Center for State Courts
300 Newport Avenue
Williamsburg, VA 23187
804-253-2000
Compiles and analyzes statistics on court-connected ADR programs around the country.

National Institute for Dispute Resolution
1726 M St., NW, Suite 500
Washington, DC 20036
202-466-4764
Information clearinghouse for dispute resolution and conflict education programs nationally.

Society of Professionals in Dispute Resolution
815 15th Street, NW, Suite 500
Washington, DC 20005
202-783-7277
Provides information on dispute resolution field, and can make recommendations to practitioners nationwide.

MEDIATION SERVICES

American Arbitration Association
140 West 51st Street
New York, NY 10020
212-484-4000
Nonprofit organization provides information and maintains extensive library on all forms of dispute resolution; sponsors training programs and administers mediation and arbitration programs through offices across the country.

Arbitration Forums, Inc.
3350 Buschwood Park Drive, Suite 295
Tampa, FL 33688
813-931-4004
800-967-8889
Nonprofit organization arbitrates and mediates commercial disputes, particularly those involving the insurance industry, through offices nationwide.

Asian Pacific American Dispute Resolution Center
1010 South Flower Street, Suite 301
Los Angeles, CA 90015
213-747-9943
Provides mediation and conciliation services in Asian Pacific languages. Handles cases involving ethnic disputes and race relations, and domestic, housing, neighborhood, employment, and business conflicts.

CDR Associates
100 Arapahoe, Suite 12
Boulder, CO 80302
303-442-7367, 800-MEDIATE
Provides extensive training programs in mediation and conflict management, and mediates major disputes involving corporations, governments, and communities nationally.

Center for Dispute Settlement
1666 Connecticut Ave., NW
Washington, DC 20009
202-265-9572
Provides general mediation and arbitration services, and training.

Dispute Resolution, Inc.
179 Allyn Street, Suite 508
Hartford, CT 06103
860-724-0861, 800-726-2393
Private dispute resolution company offers mediation and arbitration of wide range of commercial disputes.

Empire Mediation & Arbitration, Inc.
Building No. 1
625 Panorama Trail
Rochester, NY 14625
716-381-6830
Private dispute resolution firm mediates and arbitrates wide range of commercial disputes.

Federal Mediation and Conciliation Service
2100 K Street, NW
Washington, DC 20427
202-606-8080
Government agency provides information and services in connection with the resolution of labor disputes.

Institute for Christian Conciliation
1537 Avenue D, Suite 352
Billings, MT 59102
406-256-1583
Mediates disputes based on Christian biblical principles of conflict resolution, and provides conflict resolution training.

Jewish Conciliation Board of America
120 West 57th Street
New York, NY 10019
212-425-5051, ext. 3202
Provides dispute resolution services to the Jewish community on cases involving parents and children, financial matters, marital conflicts, and other issues.

Judicial Arbitration & Mediation Services, Inc./Endispute
1920 Main St., Suite 300
Irvine, CA 92714
714-224-1810, 800-352-JAMS
Largest private dispute resolution company, with offices nationwide; mediates and arbitrates wide range of commercial disputes.

The Keystone Center
P.O. Box 8606
Keystone, CO 80435
303-468-5822
Resolves public policy conflicts associated with science, technology, energy, health, and the environment.

Lesbian and Gay Community Services Center Mediation Program
208 West 13th St.
New York, NY 10011
212-620-7310, ext. 321
Program helps gay men and lesbians resolve conflicts outside the court system, including relationship breakups, child custody and visitation issues, and organizational disputes.

Resolute Systems, Inc.
15710 West Greenfield Ave., Suite 301
Brookfield, WI 53005
414-784-1595, 800-776-6060
Private dispute resolution company with five offices nationally; mediates and arbitrates wide range of commercial disputes.

Resolve, Inc.
2828 Pennsylvania Ave., NW
Washington, DC 20007
202-944-230
Specializes in resolving environmental disputes.

Settlement Consultants International Inc.
14330 Midway Road, Suite 108
Dallas, TX 75244
214-661-3771, 800-574-4744
Private dispute resolution company provides mediation and arbitration of commercial disputes, and extensive conflict resolution training.

U.S. Arbitration & Mediation, Inc.
National Administrative Office
2100 Westown Parkway, Suite 210
West Des Moines, IA 50265
800-318-2700
Network of national offices providing general mediation and arbitration of commercial disputes.

Western Network
616 Don Gaspar
Santa Fe, NM 87501
505-982-9805
Specializes in public policy disputes involving natural resources and environmental regulation and which affect relations between communities, organized interest groups, and government.

Statewide Mediation Offices

Many states now have, or are in the process of forming, special offices to coordinate mediation services within the state. Some offices are sponsored or partly funded by state governments; others are independent nonprofit organizations that assume this role themselves. These offices specialize in mediating disputes involving public policy issues, and many can also provide information on mediators and mediation services located within their states.

The following list is provided by the National Council of State Dispute Resolution Programs, of which the National Institute of Dispute Resolution serves as secretariat. For more information on any of the offices listed, contact the National Institute for Dispute Resolution, 1726 M Street, NW, Suite 500, Washington, DC 20036, 202-466-4764, ext. 312.

ALABAMA

Alabama Center for Dispute Resolution
415 Dexter Avenue
P.O. Box 671
Montgomery, AL 36101
205-269-0409

CALIFORNIA

Common Ground
Law & Public Policy Programs
University of California, Davis
Research Park
Davis, CA 95616
916-757-8569

California Center for Public Dispute Resolution
Joint Program of Calif. State Univ., Sacramento,
& McGeorge School of Law
980 Ninth Street, Suite 300
Sacramento, CA 95814
916-445-2079

COLORADO

Office of Dispute Resolution
Colorado Judicial Department
1301 Pennsylvania Street, Suite 300
Denver, CO 80203-2416
303-837-3667

FLORIDA

Florida Conflict Resolution Consortium
325 John Knox Road, Suite G-100
Tallahassee, FL 32303-4161
904-921-9069

Florida Dispute Resolution Center
Supreme Court Building
500 South Duvall Street
Tallahassee, FL 32399-1905
904-921-2910

GEORGIA

Georgia Office of Dispute Resolution
Supreme Court of Georgia
800 The Hurt Building
50 Hurt Plaza
Atlanta, GA 30303
404-527-8789

HAWAII

Center for Alternative Dispute Resolution
Office of the Admin. Dir. of the Courts
The Judiciary - State of Hawaii
P.O. Box 2560
Honolulu, HI 96804
808-539-4980

MAINE

Public Sector Dispute Resolution Project
University of Maine School of Law
246 Deering Avenue
Portland, ME 04102
207-780-4566

MASSACHUSETTS

Office of Dispute Resolution
Commonwealth of Massachusetts
Saltonstall Building, 14th Fl.
100 Cambridge Street
Boston, MA 02202
617-727-2224

MINNESOTA

Minnesota Office of Dispute Resolution
Department of Administration
304 Centennial Office Building
St. Paul, MN 55155
612-296-2633

MONTANA

Montana Consensus Council
Office of the Governor
State Capitol Building
Helena, MT 59620
406-144-2075

NEBRASKA

Office of Dispute Resolution
Supreme Court of Nebraska
Adm. Off. of the Courts/Probation
P.O. Box 98910
Lincoln, NE 68509-8910
402-471-3730

NEW HAMPSHIRE

New England Center Program on Consensus and Conflict Resolution
University of New Hampshire
11 Brookway, Rm 207
Durham, NH 03824
603-862-2232

NEW JERSEY

Office of Dispute Settlement
Department of the Sec. of State Advocate
CN 850, 25 Market Street
Trenton, NJ 08625
609-292-1773

NEW YORK

New York State Forum on Conflict & Consensus, Inc.
244 Hudson Avenue
Albany, NY 12210
518-465-2500

NORTH DAKOTA

North Dakota Consensus Council, Inc.
1003 Interstate Avenue, Suite 7
Bismarck, ND 58501-0500
701-2244588

OHIO

Ohio Commission on Dispute Resolution and Conflict Management
77 South High Street
Columbus, OH 43266-0124
614-752-9595

OREGON

Oregon Dispute Resolution Commission
1174 Chemeketa Street, NE
Salem, OR 97310
503-378-2877

TEXAS

Center for Public Policy Dispute Resolution
School of Law, Univ. of Texas at Austin
727 East 26th Street
Austin, TX 78705
512-471-3507

VERMONT

The Governor's Commission on Dispute Resolution
109 State Street, 4th Floor
Montpelier, VT 05609
802-828-3217

VIRGINIA

Dispute Resolution Services
Supreme Court of Virginia
100 North Ninth Street
Richmond, VA 23219
804-786-6455

WASHINGTON

Washington Dispute Resolution Project
Office of Financial Management
Insurance Bldg., P.O. Box 43113
Olympia, WA 98504-3113
360-586-8629

Degree and Certificate Programs in Conflict Resolution

Conflict Resolution and Mediation Education and Degree Programs

The following list will give you a sample of the many college and university programs in mediation and conflict resolution. It is not a comprehensive listing of all educational programs available, though we have tried to list the major programs. For instance, it does not include law school alternative dispute resolution programs, nor the conflict management and negotiation courses offered by many business schools. Many community colleges and university continuing education programs also offer certificates in conflict resolution and mediation; several are listed here, but of course there is no way to include them all. For more extensive listings, try these websites:
www.petersons.com
www.crinfo.org/v3-education_college.cfm
www.campus-adr.org/classroom_building/degreeprograms.html.

California

California State University, Chico:
Alternative Dispute Resolution Certificate
www.csuchico.edu/catalog/cat99/programs/pols/cert_adr.html
400 West First Street, Chico, CA 95929
530-898-5301; fax: 530-898-6910
email: pols@csuchico.edu

California State University, Dominguez Hills:
MA in Negotiation and Conflict Management
www.csudh.edu/dominguezonline/BEH.htm
1000 East Victoria Street, Carson, CA 90747
310-243-3741; fax: 310-516-3971
email: midl@csudh.edu

Fresno Pacific University, Center for Peacemaking and Conflict Studies
www.fresno.edu/pacs
1717 South Chestnut Avenue
Fresno, CA 93702
800-909-8677; fax: 559-252-4800
email: pacs@fresno.edu
Graduate degree, mediation practicum.

Golden Gate University, Ageno School of Business
www.ggu.edu/school_of_business/programs_degrees/psychology_applied_psychology/graduate_certificates
536 Mission Street, San Francisco, CA 94105
415-442-6500; fax: 415-442-6579
email: biz@ggu.edu
Graduate Certificate in Conflict Resolution.

Sonoma State University, School of Extended Education, Conflict Resolution Certificate Program
www.sonoma.edu/ExEd/certificates/cr/crindex.html
1801 East Cotati Ave., Rohnert Park, CA 94928
707-664-2394

University of California Berkeley, Extension
Mediation and Conflict Resolution Seminar
www.unex.berkeley.edu
1995 University Avenue, Berkeley, CA 94720
510-642-4111
Certificate of completion satisfies training requirements for most court and agency mediation programs.

University of California Riverside, Extension
Certificate Program in Dispute Resolution
www.unex.ucr.edu/certificates/dispute_res.html
UCR Extension Center, 1200 University Ave.
Riverside, CA 92507-4596
909-787-4111 ext. 1616
email: law@ucx.ucr.edu

Colorado

University of Denver
Conflict Resolution Program
www.du.edu/con-res
Ben Cherrington Hall, 2201 South Gaylord
Denver, CO 80208
303-871-2305; fax: 303-871-3585
email: kfeste@du.edu
MA degree program. Certificate of Advanced Study in ADR through University College.

Connecticut

University of New Haven, Department of Legal Studies, Dispute Resolution Concentration
www.newhaven.edu/psps/legalstudies.html
300 Boston Post Road, West Haven, CT 06516
203-932-7373
email: MorrisDD@charger.newhaven.edu
Undergraduate degree.

Florida

Nova Southeastern University
www.nova.edu/shss/DCAR
3100 SW 9th Avenue
Fort Lauderdale, FL 33315
800-262-7978
PhD, MS, or Graduate Certificate in Conflict Analysis and Resolution.

University of South Florida Conflict Resolution Collaborative
www.crc.usf.edu
2901 West Busch Blvd., Suite 707
Tampa, FL 33618
813-975-4816; fax: 813-975-4816
Certification programs in family and circuit civil court mediation. Approved by Florida Supreme Court.

Georgia

Brenau University, Conflict Resolution and Legal Studies Program
www.brenau.edu/sfah/humanities/CR
1 Centennial Circle, Gainesville, GA 30501
770-534-6297

Kennesaw State University, MS in Conflict Management
www.kennesaw.edu/pols/mscm
1000 Chastain Road, #2302
Kennesaw, GA 30144
770-423-6299
email: kohlsson@kennesaw.edu
Undergraduate degree also available.

Illinois

North Central College Dispute Resolution Center
www.noctrl.edu/OAO/dispute.shtml
30 North Brainard Street, P.O. Box 3063
Naperville, IL 60566
630-637-5100
Program offers training in either professional or community mediation.

Indiana

Indiana State University, Conflict Resolution Programs
http://spot.indstate.edu/crp/info.html
200 North Seventh Street
Terre Haute, IN 47809
812-237-3431; fax: 812-237-8072
MS with specialization in conflict resolution; includes mediation training. Certificate of Mediation program also available. (Offered through Department of Sociology.)

Indiana University, School of Public and Environmental Affairs
www.indiana.edu/~speaweb
1315 East Tenth Street Bloomington, IN 47405
800-765-7755; local: 812-855-2840
fax: 812-855-7802
email: speainfo@indiana.edu
Graduate certificate in Conflict Resolution.

Maryland

Salisbury University, Center for Conflict Resolution
www.conflict-resolution.org
1100 Camden Avenue
Salisbury, MD 21801
410-219-2873; fax: 410-219-2879
email: conflictresolution@salisbury.edu
Undergraduate degree in Conflict Analysis and Dispute Resolution. Community and campus mediation centers offer practical internships and training.

University of Baltimore, Center for Negotiations and Conflict Management
www.ubalt.edu/study/graduate/negotiations_conflict.html
1420 North Charles Street
Baltimore, MD 21201-5779
410-837-6566
email: dmulcahey@ubmail.ubalt.edu
Offers MS degree in Negotiations and Conflict Management.

Massachusetts

Clark University, College of Professional and Continuing Education
http://copace.clarku.edu/programs/cagsconflict.htm
950 Main Street
Worcester, MA 01610
508-793-7217
Certificate of Advanced Graduate Study in Conflict Management. For working professionals and educators with master's degrees who want to continue academic study, but don't want to get a PhD.

Lesley College School of Education, Certificate in Conflict Resolution and Peaceable Schools
www.lesley.edu/soe/ac_peaceable.html
29 Everett Street, Cambridge, MA 02138-2790
617-349-8393

University of Massachusetts at Boston, Dispute Resolution Program
www.umb.edu/academics/graduate/dispute_resolution/index.html
100 Morrissey Blvd.
Boston, MA 02125-3393
617-287-6000; fax: 617-287-6264
email: disres@umb.edu
Two graduate programs: MA in Dispute Resolution and Graduate Certificate in Dispute Resolution.

Michigan

Wayne State University, College of Urban, Labor and Metropolitan Affairs
www.culma.wayne.edu/students/madr.htm
656 W. Kirby, Room 3198, Faculty/Admin. Building
Detroit, MI 48202
313-577-3221
email: l.keashly@wayne.edu
MA and graduate certificate in dispute resolution.

New Jersey

Montclair State University, Concentration in Dispute Resolution
www.chss.montclair.edu/leclair/LS/dr.html
Department of Legal Studies, College of Humanities and Social Sciences
Upper Montclair, NJ 07043
973-655-7292; fax: 973-655-7951

New York

City University of New York, Dispute Resolution Consortium
John Jay College of Criminal Justice, Certificate in Dispute Resolution
http://johnjay.jjay.cuny.edu/dispute
899 Tenth Avenue, Room 520
New York, NY 10019
212-237-8692; fax: 212-237-8646
email: dispute@jjay.cuny.edu
Certificate authorized by the City University of New York and the New York State Department of Education. Website has extensive links to education and training resources for New York City and state.

Columbia University Teachers College, Conflict Resolution Certificate
www.tc.edu/icccr
525 West 120th St.
New York, NY 10027-6696
212-678-3710
email: tcinfo@www.tc.columbia.edu

Ohio

Antioch University McGregor
www.mcgregor.edu/cr
800 Livermore Street
Yellow Springs, OH 45387
937-769-1800
MA in conflict resolution. Advanced Mediator Training Institute for practicing mediators.

Kent State University, Center for Applied Conflict Management
http://dept.kent.edu/cacm
P.O. Box 5190, 302 Bowman Hall
Kent, OH 44242-0001
330-672-3143; fax: 330-672-3362
Offers undergraduate degree.

University of Akron, Center for Conflict Management
http://gozips.uakron.edu/~conmang
Leigh Hall 201
Akron, OH 44325-6234
330-972-7008; fax: 330-972-5263
Offers certificate and degree in conflict resolution.

Oregon

Portland State University, School of Extended Studies, Program in Negotiation and Mediation
www.ceed.pdx.edu/neg_n_med.shtml
P.O. Box 1491
Portland, OR 97207
800-547-8887 ext 4876; local: 503-725-4876
email: sharpml@pdx.edu
Meets the requirements of the Oregon Dispute Resolution Commission's basic mediation curriculum.

Southern Oregon University, Extended Campus Programs, Certificate Program in Dispute Resolution
www.sou.edu/ecp/business/mediation/index.html
1250 Siskiyou Blvd.
Ashland, OR 97520
541-552-6334; fax: 541-552-6047

Pennsylvania

Duquesne University, Graduate Center for Social and Public Policy
www.policycenter.duq.edu/cert.html
550A College Hall, 600 Forbes Avenue
Pittsburgh, PA 15282
412-396-1780; fax: 412-396-1739
email: socialpolicy@duq.edu
Graduate certificate in conflict resolution and peace studies.

South Carolina

Columbia College, Graduate Program in Human Behavior and Conflict Management
www.columbiacollegesc.edu/graduate/conflict.html
1301 Columbia College Drive
Columbia SC 29203
800-277-1301

Texas

St. Edward's University, MA in Human Services
www.stedwards.edu/mahs/conflict.htm
3001 South Congress Avenue
Austin, TX 78704
512-448-8400
Develops qualified mediators for human services agencies and organizations. Students must have trained supervisors, managers, and administrators. Specialization in Conflict Resolution.

Southern Methodist University, Continuing Education, Dispute Resolution Certificate Program
www.smu.edu/continuing_education/professional/disputeresolution
5228 Tennyson Parkway, Suite 118
Plano, TX 75024
972-473-3439; fax: 972-473-3441

Texas Woman's University, Continuing Education, Certificate Program in Conflict Resolution
www.twu.edu/o-ll/Mediation.htm
P.O. Box 425649
Denton, TX 76204
940-898-3408; fax: 940-898-3416

Utah

University of Utah, Department of Communication, Conflict Resolution Certificate Program
www.hum.utah.edu/communication/certificate/conres.html
255 South Central Campus Drive
Room LNCO 2810
Salt Lake City, UT 84112
801-585-9662
Satisfies the educational requirement for Utah state certification as a mediator and a negotiator. (Graduate degree also available.)

Vermont

Woodbury College, Mediation and Conflict Management Program
www.woodbury-college.edu/prospective/mediation.html
660 Elm Street
Montpelier, VT 05602
800-639-6039; fax: 802-229-2141
email: kathleen@woodbury-college.edu
Thirty-one-week comprehensive training program.

Virginia

George Mason University, Institute for Conflict Analysis and Resolution
http://web.gmu.edu/departments/icar
4260 Chain Bridge Road (Route 123)
Fairfax, VA 22030
703-993-1300; fax: 703-993-1302
MS and PhD programs in conflict resolution. Certificate in conflict resolution for health professionals.

James Madison University: Conflict and Mediation Studies
www.jmu.edu/commstudies/cmstudies.htm
800 South Main Street, Anthony-Seeger 28
Harrisonburg, VA 22807
540-568-6228
email: kimseywd@jmu.edu
Undergraduate degree. Also runs a mediation center.

Wisconsin

Marquette University, Center for Dispute Resolution Education
www.marquette.edu/disputeres
P.O. Box 1881, Wehr Physics, Room 107
Milwaukee, WI 53201
414-288-5535; fax: 414-288-1902
email: dispute.resolution @marquette.edu
Graduate certificate in dispute resolution.

University of Wisconsin, Continuing Studies Dept. of Professional Development and Applied Studies
www.dcs.wisc.edu/pda/hhi/mediation/default.htm
610 Langdon Street, Room 313
Madison, WI 53703
608-263-2088; fax: 608-265-2329
Workshops and training in mediation and dispute resolution, including divorce mediation.

University of Wisconsin, Parkside, Certificate in Conflict Analysis & Resolution
http://oldweb.uwp.edu/academic/communication/classes/shailor/conflictpages
900 Wood Road, P.O. Box 2000
Kenosha, WI 53141
414-595-2218

Other

University of Phoenix
Professional Certificate Programs
www.uophx.edu/Allother_Campusesprograms/conres.html
800-697-8223
Professional certificates in Alternative Dispute Resolution, Art of Negotiation, and Conflict Resolution (offered at various campus locations).

Index

A

B

C

D

N

T

U

V

W

more from

NOLO

Law for All

Represent Yourself in Court

How to Prepare & Try a Winning Case

by Attorneys Paul Bergman & Sara Berman-Barrett

You can be heard and taken seriously in any courtroom. And with this book, you'll be well prepared to achieve great results, without having to pay a lawyer's ransom! This book will help you handle a divorce, landlord/tenant conflict, breach of contract, small-business dispute or any other civil lawsuit.

$34.99/RYC

The Lawsuit Survival Guide

A Client's Companion to Litigation

by Attorney Joseph Matthews

The Lawsuit Survival Guide takes you through the entire civil litigation process from start to finish, explaining every step along the way in language that makes sense. It will save you and your lawyer time, money and aggravation—and give you the information you need to make smart lawsuit decisions.

$29.99/UNCL

Everybody's Guide to Small Claims Court

by Attorney Ralph Warner

Go after the money that's owed you—represent yourself in small claims court and win! Use the step-by-step instructions in *Everybody's Guide to Small Claims Court* to successfully present your case, whether it concerns an auto repair, rental deposit, property damage, small business dispute and more.

$26.99/NSCC

How to Win Your Personal Injury Claim

by Attorney Joseph Matthews

How to Win Your Personal Injury Claim is filled with strategies for handling every stage of the insurance-claim process, providing all the information you need to evaluate how much your claim is worth, bargain with insurance companies, and obtain a full and fair settlement. Includes checklists, worksheets and step-by-step instructions.

$29.99/PICL

800-728-3555 *or* **www.nolo.com**

Remember:

Little publishers have big ears.
We really listen to you.

Take 2 Minutes & Give Us Your 2 cents

Your comments make a big difference in the development and revision of Nolo books and software. Please take a few minutes and register your Nolo product—and your comments—with us. Not only will your input make a difference, you'll receive special offers available only to registered owners of Nolo products on our newest books and software. Register now by:

PHONE
1-800-728-3555

FAX
1-800-645-0895

EMAIL
cs@nolo.com

or **MAIL** us
this registration card

fold here

NOLO

Registration Card

NAME ______________________ DATE ______________________

ADDRESS ______________________

____

CITY ______________________ STATE __________ ZIP __________

PHONE ______________________ EMAIL ______________________

WHERE DID YOU HEAR ABOUT THIS PRODUCT? ______________________

WHERE DID YOU PURCHASE THIS PRODUCT? ______________________

DID YOU CONSULT A LAWYER? (PLEASE CIRCLE ONE) YES NO NOT APPLICABLE

DID YOU FIND THIS BOOK HELPFUL? (VERY) 5 4 3 2 1 (NOT AT ALL)

COMMENTS ______________________

____

____

WAS IT EASY TO USE? (VERY EASY) 5 4 3 2 1 (VERY DIFFICULT)

We occasionally make our mailing list available to carefully selected companies whose products may be of interest to you.

❑ If you do not wish to receive mailings from these companies, please check this box.

❑ You can quote me in future Nolo promotional materials.
Daytime phone number ______________________.

BECM 1.0

"Nolo helps lay people perform legal tasks without the aid—or fees—of lawyers."

—USA TODAY

Nolo books are ..."written in plain language, free of legal mumbo jumbo, and spiced with witty personal observations."

—ASSOCIATED PRESS

"...Nolo publications...guide people simply through the how, when, where and why of law."

—WASHINGTON POST

"Increasingly, people who are not lawyers are performing tasks usually regarded as legal work... And consumers, using books like Nolo's, do routine legal work themselves."

—NEW YORK TIMES

"...All of [Nolo's] books are easy-to-understand, are updated regularly, provide pull-out forms...and are often quite moving in their sense of compassion for the struggles of the lay reader."

—SAN FRANCISCO CHRONICLE

fold here

Place stamp here

Attn: BECM 1.0